The Greatest Guide to

Green Living

This is a **GREATEST**GUIDES title

Greatest Guides Limited, Woodstock, Bridge End, Warwick CV34 6PD, United Kingdom

www.greatestguides.com

Series created by Harshad Kotecha

Greatest Guides is committed to a sustainable future for our planet. This book is printed on paper certified by the Forest Stewardship Council.

MIX
Paper
FSC   FSC® C020837

Printed and bound in the United Kingdom

ISBN 978-1-907906-08-4

I would like to thank the following for their invaluable help in providing tips, for proofreading and for their support.

Jon – my long suffering fiancé, who's proofreading skills are second to none.

My Mum (Beryl) and Valerie (almost Mother-in-law) for their supply of relevant magazine and newspaper cuttings.

Contents

A few words from Lynne...

As more and more of us become aware of the effect we have on the earth, we are beginning to understand that we must do something to lessen that impact. This book is, therefore, aimed at those who realize we should make alterations but are unable to sell up and move to a self-sufficient one hundred acre farm in the middle of nowhere. The tips and hints included within are easily incorporated into your lives, so why not commit to making just one change a week? Then you'll be getting nearer to your goal with each tiny step, that of living a life that has less impact on this fragile planet.

I have always been a 'greenie' but, like many, knowing and doing are two different things. However, since researching this book I have made changes, which include:

- Placing water filled bottles into toilet cisterns, to cut down on water usage.

- Dragging out the old University bike and riding it into town, although, I admit, not when it rains!

- Collecting stamps and used printer cartridges, which help raise money for worthy causes.

- Fruit and vegetables have never seen the inside of a plane. Also, if I can't buy air mile free flowers then I don't buy flowers!

- Meat comes from the local butcher who can tell me exactly what farm it came from.

- My eggs travel just 14 miles (22.5km), my honey just 4½ miles (7.25km) and I've even had some success growing a few vegetables in the back garden.

- All clothes and unwanted items are taken to a local charity shop.

- I no longer buy new books (novels) but buy from a local charity book shop or second hand book shop. Once read, they are returned and replaced with new second hand reads.

- Our bin has gone on a diet and now much of our food goes into the composter.

- I've learnt to cook pizza, Mexican and Chinese, so we know exactly what has gone into them. This also cuts down on packaging and the petrol required for home delivery.

- I've discovered the delights of cleaning with bicarbonate of soda and vinegar.

All these small changes have been easily built into our daily lives. Yes we slip every so often, but those slips are getting few and far between.

So join the ranks and see if we can make the changes that are needed together.

Lynne

Your Pets

66 The most important fact about Spaceship Earth: an instruction book didn't come with it. 99

R. Buckminster Fuller (1895-1983)

Chapter 1
Your Pets

Pets share our lives and are often a member of the family. However, the sad fact is that they also have an impact on the environment, either through their actions or the actions we take on their behalf. So don't leave them out of your endeavors in becoming green. A few simple changes to your habits will help.

Pick up that poop

Today we are aware of the health hazard poop poses. The new problem is that many of us use plastic bags to pick it up. These then go into a bin which is eventually added to the landfill time bomb. Rather than using plastic bags that do not degrade, try using biodegradable bags or bags that can be flushed down the toilet. These bags and the dog waste are treated in exactly the same way as human waste. If you're unable to find a local stockist, then simply type in 'flushable pooper scooper bags' in any search engine. Alternatively, why not invest in a doggie loo? These are sunk into the ground (in your garden) and break down the waste into a harmless 'slush' that filters into the surrounding soil. However, do ensure that the lid is secure otherwise these can be death-traps for passing wildlife.

Au naturelle

According to the Cancer Prevention Coalition (CPC), the ingredients on some flea collars are carcinogens, neurotoxins or both. So why not try natural repellents like essential oils? Simply purchase an absorbent woven collar and, using a dropper, place a couple of drops of your chosen oil onto the collar (never directly onto your pet's skin). Essential oils that repel fleas and ticks include citronella (dogs only), rosemary and rose geranium; repeat the process weekly. Take care with the first few applications, ensuring your pet is okay with the strong, unfamiliar smell.

Whoops!

Whether young or old, our pets sometimes have little accidents. If we're lucky, they're on a hard surface so are easy to clean up. But if they happen on carpets, cleaning can be difficult. Rather than reaching for those nasty chemicals give baking soda or vinegar a go. First sprinkle the area with baking soda and allow it to do its stuff overnight, and then remove. Then mix one cup of strong white vinegar with half a gallon of water and wash the area. Before using any new cleaning method always do a spot check on a piece of carpet that is normally hidden under furniture.

GREEN FACT

In the US, it is estimated that for every 415 human babies born 5,500 puppies and kittens are born.

Play time

Rather than spend your money on expensive plastic toys that have been shipped across oceans, why not try to find cheap, natural alternatives? Our pooch loves to run around with or cuddle a piece of rag (often made from an old tea-towel or pillowcase) with a knot at both ends. This toy also provides hours of fun as it is used for tug-of-war games.

Food for thought

Whilst researching pet food, I was shocked to learn that many pet food manufacturers use meat (this is a very loose term) that comes from animals that are classed as 4-D, which stands for dead, dying, diseased or disabled. Once I found this out I invested in a couple of doggy cook books. The chicken liver treats I now bake go down so well that I can't have them in my pocket when I go dog walking otherwise I end up looking like the Pied Piper!

Tag, you're it!

You may wonder why I'm advocating getting your friend tagged. Well think about it. They wander off, so what do you do? You put up posters and spend hours driving around looking for them. This uses paper, ink and fuel. So a tag (obviously made from recycled materials) or a microchip will help reunite you quicker.

At the end

It's a sad fact of life that our pets die. Many of us would simply throw out their belongings. But think twice before you do. That rabbit hutch would be a great new home for a wildlife casualty being cared for by a local rescue center, that uneaten food will cut the food bills at a local shelter. A quick call to your local veterinary practice or a look in your local phone book will supply a number of good homes for those unwanted items.

Itchy problem

Fleas and ticks can be a problem and can cause health issues, such as Lyme Disease. So rather than spray or bathe them with chemicals, why not try a couple of cloves of garlic a day hidden in food? Garlic is also good for the blood and digestion, although you may wish to make them some mint biscuits to sort out the continental 'doggy' breath.

Help others

Believe it or not, you can help save the life of someone else's pet by donating blood to a blood bank. Over the last few years more and more veterinary practices are joining schemes and will hold special blood donation days. Simply give your vet a call to find out if your pet would be eligible to take part or search online for a local scheme.

" Our environment, the world in which we live and work, is a mirror of our attitudes and expectations. "

Earl Nightingale

Little porky

It's a shame but many of our pets are suffering from the blight of obesity. Unless they have a medical condition, most overweight pets are this way because they eat too much. The production of this food is a drain on natural resources. Along with this weight problem can come health problems, which use yet more resources. So give them a little less food and a little more walking and help the planet.

Tinker bell

Each year thousands of little lives are lost to the preying habits of our pets, mainly cats. By fitting your cat's collar with a bell, you will give all those little feathered and furry friends a fighting chance. It'll also cut down on the stress of finding disemboweled creatures on your carpet!

Bath time

We seem to have a thing about being clean, which is not a problem on its own but it has meant that more water and bath products are being used. This clean 'thing' has also increased the number of baths we give our pets. Now, unless they really, really need it because they've rolled in something gross, the answer is simple: have fewer bath times, something most pets will be more than delighted to hear about!

Grow your own

A whole range of items for bathing, eating and turning into toys (catnip bags for example) are easy to grow. So why not have a go at growing:

Wheat Grass

Soak grains of wheat overnight. Drain (saving the water obviously), place the grains in a seed tray with a small amount of space between each then cover with 1/4" (2 – 4mm) of soil and water daily, ensuring the soil is very slightly moist. When it reaches 4" (10cm) tall cut and add to food or allow your pet to eat straight from the tray.

Catnip

Catnip is easy to grow and, with the addition of a little fabric, can be used to create little bags of fun for your cat. It should be started indoors early in the year and once the chance of frost has passed it can be transplanted outside. Place the seeds in a seed tray then cover with 1/4" (2 – 4mm) of soil and water daily, ensuring the soil is slightly moist. Once the seedlings are big enough transplant them outside leaving 12" (30cm) between each one. Indoors, they prefer direct light, if you are providing light then ensure the light is 2"– 4" (5cm –10cm) above the top of the plant. Catnip loves water so you should ensure the soil never dries out. To harvest and dry, ensure the leaves are fully grown and dry them by hanging them upside down in a warm dry environment. When the leaves are dried and crunchy they can be crumbled and used to bring joy to your cat.

Garlic

Garlic is great for getting rid of worms; strengthening the digestion and can cut down on biting insects, such as ticks and fleas. To grow: pick a bulb that is fresh, plump and firm with the papery skin still in place. Break the bulb into the individual cloves then plant each one with the point up. They will grow in most good soils in a warm bright position, just remember to ensure the soil is kept moist.

Parsley

Great for adding to home made biscuits, which freshens breath. This is perhaps best grown in a pot as it prefers rich soil and full sunlight. So if you have a window sill that suits, then you're half way there. Sow in early spring in a pot and keep the soil damp. Once the seedlings are 3"– 4" (8 cm – 10cm) tall they can be placed outside. When placing outside, dig holes and add organic matter and bone meal to the top layer of soil. Remember to water once a month using a fertilizer to ensure good growth. Parsley can be harvested up until it starts to produce seeds, which can then be used for your next crop.

Mint

Great for adding to home made biscuits for freshening breath. If you plan to grow this herb then perhaps a container would be the best option as it is a very invasive plant and can overtake your garden. Mint prefers partial shade and soil that is moist, moderately rich and slightly acidic. It is difficult to grow from seed so you may want to invest in some small plants you can bring on. You can harvest as and when needed and, in order to increase growth, pinch the stem ends off each sprig. If you want to grow in the garden then place in a large hole-less container and sink this into the ground.

Lavender

There are 50 different species of Lavender, with many widely available from good garden centres. Each one has a slightly different preference so ensure you pick one that is suitable for where you live. When digging in add some compost to the hole and plant out early autumn or mid-spring. If you want your plant to become bushing, then pinch out the tops of leaves and stalks. Take care not to overwater and feed once a year. To harvest, cut in the morning when the buds are not fully open, create a bundle held together with an elastic band and hang upside down in a cool, dry dark place. This drying process should take a couple of weeks. Once completely dry, place the bundle over a bowl and rub your hands down the length of the lavender to remove the buds, which you can then use.

Cat Grass

Place the seeds in a container with drainage holes and fill with multi-purpose compost. Sprinkle the seeds over the compost then sprinkle compost thinly over the seeds. Water using a fine rose, so you don't wash away the seeds, and place on a window sill. Within a couple of weeks you'll have a lovely batch of fresh new grass for your cat. Trim back on a regular basis to encourage the grass to keep growing.

Vegetables

Many cats and dogs like and benefit from eating raw vegetables. Not only are they better for them than shop purchased treats, but they also give mental and physical exercise and clean their teeth at the same time. Our first dog just loved raw carrots and, when offered a shop purchased chew or a carrot, she always picked the carrot first. Although, she would always come back looking for the chew to see if it was still on offer. To find out more about feeding vegetables to your cats and dogs, check out some of the books listed in the 'Books for your Library' section.

" We could have saved the Earth but we were too damned cheap. "

Kurt Vonnegut, Jr.

Get the snip

Animals will do what animals do, which includes making baby animals. Each year, thousands of unwanted pets are put to sleep, given to animal shelters or simply thrown onto the street because of an unwanted pregnancy. So get your cat or dog neutered. Not only is it environmentally sound but you'll also not have to go through the trauma of trying to find homes for those adorable little kittens and puppies.

GREEN FACT

During the 17th Century, if you saw a cat washing its face it was seen as a sign of a storm brewing. If you saw a black cat it would bring you bad luck and if you saw a white cat at night the Grim Reaper was on his way. If you heard a dog howling at night bad luck was on its way, however, if a dog licked the face of a newborn that baby would be a fast healer.

The flight of the flea

Once you've solved the problem of fleas on your pet, your next task is to ensure they're not hiding in your home. There are several ways you can achieve this. Firstly vacuum soft furnishings and cracks in floors, etc. during the height of the flea season. Once this has been done, if your cleaner has a bag, clean it immediately as the eggs can hatch in there. Fleas don't like mint, rosemary, cedar, and lavender, so make yourself a few small bags of these and hide them down the side of your sofa and chair cushions.

Up and down

Dogs and cats feel the heat just like we do but they don't have the opportunity to 'peel' off those layers when it's hot indoors. So, during the winter, wear an extra layer and turn the thermostat down three degrees and if you have air conditioning turn it three degrees up. If all households were to do this it's estimated 1,000lb (500kg) less CO_2 will be created in the UK alone. So it's not only good for the environment but should also cut down on the loss of hair from your furry friends due to overheating.

> **Take care of the earth and she will take care of you.**
>
> Author Unknown

Drug bust

If your pet has been treated by the vet dispose of any leftover drugs with care once the treatment is finished. The best solution is to return them to your vet, who will dispose of them for you.

Pesky plastic

Many pet items are made from plastic, some of which have been linked to health issues (for example: thyroid disease in cats). So try to use bedding and toys made from natural materials that have been grown organically and invest in feeding bowls made from stainless steel.

Something a little different

If you're looking for a pet that's a little different (but not exotic) then why not try a couple of chickens? You can 'recycle' a chicken by providing a home for an ex-battery chicken. Although they're not suitable for living indoors, they do have the benefit that you'll be able to supplement their diet with kitchen scraps. Also, once they are fighting fit, you may even get the odd egg or two. To find a local organization, type in 'rehoming battery chickens' in your chosen search engine.

Bed time

Rather than spending loads on a bed, why not have a go at making your own? Try:

http://lifehacker.com or http://tipnut.com and type 'pet bed' into the search field. However, if you're not a sewer, a simple bed can be created by using an old quilt and quilt cover. Our pooch loves her old quilt, which has a range of covers, all purchased from the local charity shop.

Don't go tropical

Why go tropical when you can keep cold water fish? Think of all that energy you'll be saving. Also, the tropical fish pet trade has been blamed (rightly or wrongly) for damaging our coral reefs. And some traders are, to say the least, rogues! For example, did you know that there is a practice of dyeing fish so they are more saleable? Fish are injected with dye, or bleached then put into dye, and, shockingly, 80% of fish treated in this way die within days. So research the fish you want first so you know what they are supposed to look like. Names to avoid include Bubblegum Parrot or Jelly Bean, Blueberry Oscars, Fruit Tetras, Painted Cory, Painted Botia and Painted Glassfish. Also, if you see the word 'painted', steer clear of that fish!

Fish 'des-res'

Many fish love places to hide. However, care has to be taken when choosing something suitable. Make sure what you pick has not damaged the environment it was taken from, coral for example. Also, make sure it won't give off toxins that could slowly kill your fish. If you provide real plants, they will oxygenate the water rather than you having to use a bubble-making accessory.

Chauffeur service

It's amazing how many pampered pets enjoy a small car ride. If they need to go somewhere, the pet parlour for example, try find one that is within walking distance so you don't have to use the car or why not join forces with a friend and car share. Also check to ensure they have the same high standards as you do when it comes to environmental concerns. There's little point in being 'good' at home if you then support a business that doesn't have the same values.

Worms

We've already suggested alternate pets in the form of chickens but, if you have young kids, why not go for worms? Your first reaction will be Yuk! But kids love Yuk! And the great thing about these pets is that they'll convert all that nasty kitchen waste into compost. Simply put worm farming into your chosen search engine to find a local supplier.

66 We shall require a substantially new manner of thinking if mankind is to survive. **99**

Albert Einstein

Out and about

When you get the chance to have a wild night out, don't be tempted to leave all the lights on in the house. Pets see better than we do in dim light, so leaving lights on is pointless.

Accessorize

Our pets seem to need so much: a bed, a collar, toys, towels, some people even dress their furry friends. The production of these 'must haves' has an impact, so try to lessen this by buying items that use organically grown products, such as cotton or hemp, or recycled items, such as recycled PET bottles.

Mix it up

In a feature published by Time Magazine (1994), it was estimated that 25% of all purebred dogs were suffering from serious genetic problems from too much interbreeding. This is not only unpleasant for the dogs but also increases the chances of having to resort to medicines and medical procedures to help them, all of which are a drain on resources. However, there has been a move towards more responsible breeding, where these problems are bred out. But, when looking for a new pet, why not have a look at a local rescue center first or if you really would like a pure bred then research the breeder first to ensure they ethically breed to reduce problems rather than increase them.

Can you recycle?

Many dry pet foods come in cardboard boxes or bags. Unfortunately, some pet food boxes are lined with metal or plastic so cannot be recycled. So before you buy, read the packaging to check if it can be recycled. If it's not then don't buy it, and let the manufacturer know why you didn't buy their product. They'll not mend their ways if you don't let them know by hitting them where it hurts, their income stream.

" Waste is wrong… If everyone took that view, it really would make a difference. **"**

Sir David Attenborough

Litter bug!

It has been estimated that 35% of cats are kept indoors. This means the dreaded litter tray. Now, did you know that many cat litters are made from clay (known as diatomaceous earth or sodium bentonite) and much of this is strip mined? This lays waste to thousands upon thousands of acres of land. There are alternatives, which include recycled newspaper that has been compressed into pellets and ground corn cobs. So next time you have to stock up on litter for the tray, read the label.

Exotic fads

Exotic seems to mean fashionable or hip when it comes to pets. But before you purchase such a friend, think! It may be cool to make your friends skin crawl as you hoist out the 2 meter Boa constrictor from it's tank but is it environmentally sound? You'd be shocked by how many exotic animals and birds are still caught in the wild and then shipped from their native lands. Surely a plain old rabbit or hamster (from the local shelter) would give just as much enjoyment. If you'd like to find out more about how the exotic pet trade effects wildlife populations, then check out **www.traffic.org**

Brush, brush, brush

Many pets moult on a continual basis, forming great clumps of hair, which we call tumbleweed in our house. Rather than resorting to vacuuming, invest in a broom to remove the unsightly hair on wood, lino, tile or laminate flooring. However, if you solve the problem at the source you'll save yourself a job. Now I'm not suggesting you completely shave your pet, but a good brush each day will be beneficial to you both. And don't throw that unwanted hair away. You could perhaps take up knitting; yes, there are even a couple of books on knitting with dog hair (Knitting with Dog Hair: Better a Sweater from a Dog You Know and Love Than from a Sheep You'll Never Meet by Kendall Crolius and Anne Montgomery or Knitting with Dog Hair: A Woof-To-Warp Guide to Making Hats, Sweaters, Mittens and Much More by Kendall Crolius and Anne Black Montgomery). Or why not help the local bird population to build their nests by placing the hair in a mesh bag and hanging it on a tree or bush.

GREEN FACT

On average, our feline friends kill 40 wild animals a year each, having a drastic impact on our wildlife population.

The Garden

" Weeds are flowers too, once you get to know them. "

Eeyore, From A. A. Milne's Winnie the Pooh

Chapter 2
The Garden

For many, our gardens say as much about us as our homes do. They range from small plots to acres upon acres (if we're lucky) but they're not just ours. We tend to forget that our garden is also the home to all sorts of critters. Many of these creatures we never see, they are either too small or they use the garden when we're not there. So gardens are something we have to learn to sh… sh… share and take pleasure in the fact that we are sharing.

Back garden workout

Once upon a time, long, long ago, gardens were kept tidy without the use of electricity. So next time you decide you need a new lawnmower, go for a manual one and cut down on the amount of electricity you use. You'll not only be doing your bit for the planet but each time you cut the grass you'll also be giving yourself a great workout.

The lazy lawn

Cut down on the amount of mowing you do by simply cutting down the amount of lawn you have. Apart from widening the flower borders, you could always turn part of your lawn into a wildflower lawn. Many companies sell seeds that will provide you with a lawn full of native wild flowers. You'll not only save yourself time but will also offer a food source to many a grateful bee or butterfly.

Create from cast-offs

For those of us who don't have large gardens but want to fill them with wonderful plants, containers are the answer. Although they take a lot of care, they also allow you to be creative. Rather than popping down to the local garden center, look around to see if there is anything that can be used as an alternative; perhaps an old sink, a chimney pot, even an old watering can. Go on, get creative!

For peat's sake

Peat bogs are a rapidly vanishing and important natural habitat. The worrying fact is that over half the peat purchased is done so by the gardener. To make a difference, all you have to do is read the label. If it is peat-free it'll say so. If it used waste or recycled materials, it'll say so. Then make a purchase based on these facts. The manufacturers will soon get the idea when the sale of peat-free or recycled materials goes up and peat-based products go down.

GREEN FACT

It has been estimated that a single flower meadow can support 100 to 150 different species, big and small.

Read all about it

If you grow from seed then you'll save yourself some cash by making your own little seed pots. A great little device called the paper potter allows you to simply and easily turn newspaper into pots. Once your seedlings are ready for planting out, simply leave them in the newspaper pot and, as your plant grows, the pot will degrade naturally into compost.

Butt out!

If you're going to have a bath then don't pull the plug, use it to water your plants (as long as you didn't add bubble bath, etc.) Another great idea is to

Top wildlife attracting plants

If, like me, you are a wildlife-loving gardener, then you will definitely want some (or all!) of these plants in your garden…

- Allium hollandicum 'Purple Sensation' (Ornamental onion)
- Aster novae-angliae (Michaelmas daisy)
- Berberis darwinii (Barberry)
- Buddleia davidii (Butterfly bush)
- Caryopteris clandonensis
- Cotoneaster 'Coral Beauty'
- Digitalis species (Foxgloves)
- Echinops species (Globe thistle)
- Eryngium species (Sea holly)
- Lavender angustifolia 'Hidcote' (English lavender)
- Lavender stoechas (French lavender)
- Malus 'Red Jade' (Weeping crab apple)
- Marjoram (Oregano)
- Nepeta sibirica (Catmint)
- Philadelphus 'Beauclerk' (Mock orange)
- Rosa Canina (Dog rose)
- Salvia officinalis (Sage)
- Santolina chamaecyparissus 'Small Ness' (Cotton lavender)
- Scabiosa species (Scabious)
- Sedum spectabile (Ice plant)

invest in a water butt. Simply attach it to the guttering and you can collect all that lovely rain and use it to keep your plants alive during dry spells.

Power of the sun

Why waste electricity to light your garden paths when the sun can do it for you? If you want to have those pretty lights dotted around the garden then purchase solar powered lights. They do the job just as well as conventional plug-in lights and won't cost the earth to run. You can also get solar powered water fountains for your pond. So go on, make the sun work for you!

The green, green grass

In many cities and towns, people are resorting to turning their once lovely lawn into places to park their car. This may cut down the frustration of where to park but where will all our wildlife go? Resist the urge and let your garden become a haven for wildlife, both big and small. Make your garden one of the few in your street where people will stop, look over your fence, and wish they'd had the foresight to keep it green.

Pond life

Even the smallest of ponds can help wildlife. I have a pond the rest of my family call my puddle. However, the joy it gave me to see four dragonflies emerge as nymphs and fly off some hours later, once they had transformed, was terrific. You just have to remember that for a wildlife pond you have to resist putting in fish. Ponds are also great educational tools for kids. It not only allows you to educate them in how to act around water, but pond dipping is a must for any kid! Arm them with a good net, a large container and a book on bugs and they'll have hours of fun. Oh! And of course, if your pond has steep sides make sure you incorporate an escape ladder for creatures that fall in.

" When you use a manual
push mower, you're 'cutting' down
on pollution and the only thing
in danger of running out of gas
is you! **"**

Grey Livingston

Homes in your garden

Rather then just growing lovely flowers to attract insects, birds and mammals, why not supply a home or two as well? These can easily be purchased or, better still, if you are handy with a hammer and saw you could make your own from reclaimed wood (steer clear of treated wood just in case). Once sited, someone will quickly move in, you may be surprised at just how quickly. A few years ago I installed a bird box and a pair of blue tits moved in within 10 days! Later in the year I was blessed with baby blue tits stretching their wings and learning how to fly in my garden.

A little bit higher now

Does it really matter if your grass is slightly longer than next doors? Did you know that if you have slightly longer grass, you cut down on water evaporation? So next time you cut the grass, set the lawn mover blades one or two notches higher.

Water, water everywhere

If you really have to water your plants then there are a couple of ways to lessen the amount you use. Firstly, water at the coolest part of the day as this will reduce evaporation, and only water the parts of the garden that really, really need it. If you use a trigger nozzle rather than a sprinkler, this will also cut down waste.

Grass is greener

If you get the chance to 'restart' your lawn, use native grass seeds as they grow better and are less likely to succumb to local 'pests.' If a nasty weed pops its head up in the middle of your lawn, reach for a trowel or fork rather than weed killer, and when you cut your grass leave the cuttings in place, so the nutrients locked up in the blades of grass will return to the soil.

Keep it local

Not all plants will grow in all parts of the country, so, when planting, ensure you plant something that is suitable for your region. Have a quick chat with the local garden center, picking a day and time to visit when you'll be just one of a few rather than one of a hundred, that way they'll have time to chat. Alternatively, chat over the fence with your neighbor and ask them about the plants they've successfully grown in their garden and those they have avoided.

A rose by any other name

When choosing flowering plants, pick specimens that will attract and provide food for bees and butterflies. But don't forget that butterflies lay eggs that turn into caterpillars who will need food. For example, why not grow a couple of lettuce just for the cabbage white butterfly or allow the nettles to grow down the back of the shed for a whole range of creepy crawlies to feast on?

Decking, don't do it!

Decking is all the rage. However, think carefully about the impact this will have, not only on your garden but also the consequences of the materials you use. Ensure that it is made from recycled materials or, if you do use wood, that it comes from renewable, sustainable sources.

Water features

Many of us love to hear the sound of trickling water. However, using an electrical fountain uses energy. So invest in a solar powered fountain; these can be easily sourced at many garden or DIY centers.

Don't fence me in

Rather than a boring old wooden fence why not have a living fence and grow a hedge (using native species obviously), or a tree border (again native, don't forget the fruits they'll produce in the autumn), or why not get a wall built from reclaimed bricks? The nooks and crannies will provide new homes for little garden beasties.

Rock garden

When choosing rocks for your garden, be aware of where they have come from. Many areas of the world have lost valuable habitat due to man removing stones and rocks to make our gardens pretty. So try to source alternatives, such as reclaimed stone or sandstone.

No smoke without fire

Try to avoid lighting bonfires as they can give off harmful chemicals and release CO_2. Also be aware that a pile of sticks will look like a great new home and something can move in. If you do have to create a bonfire, then burn it on the same day you build it. If this is not possible, then check it carefully before striking that match.

Tire tower

If you love spuds but don't have the room for an allotment, pop down to the local car wreckers and get yourself a few old tires. Place a tire on the ground and plant some seed potatoes under 2" (10 cm) of compost. When the plants are 8" (20cm) tall place another tire on the top and fill it with compost so 2" (5cm) of the stems are left above the compost. Repeat until you have five tires in your tower. Then stand back, water as needed, and let those spuds grow.

Add a little extra

When you've got your first 'crop' of compost and you're ready to add it to your garden, give it a little boost by adding bone meal, stone meal or wood ash.

❝ A perfect summer day is when the sun is shining, the breeze is blowing, the birds are singing, and the lawn mower is broken. ❞

James Dent

Pesky pests

As well as the dreaded snails and slugs, our gardens can be a battleground when it comes to greenfly and the like. Rather than reaching for that chemical spray, give natural penetrators a go. For example, many 'green' gardening centers sell ladybugs and lacewings. When releasing such predators, make sure they'd appear naturally in your area (introduced species can do a lot of damage) and check that they'll only eat what you want them to get rid of.

Time to hoe

Keep an eye on the weather and next time the weather man (or woman) says it's going to rain, go out with your hoe and break the surface soil around plants. During dry weather the soil will become hardened and a crust will form. By breaking up this crust, you help the forthcoming rain penetrate through to the lower levels in the soil rather than becoming run off.

Give me your lolly

The next time the sun is out and you treat everyone to an ice lolly, don't throw away those lolly sticks, they make great plant markers when you're growing your own plants.

Cat-astrophe

If you find your garden is always full of cats, the next time you peel yourself an orange don't throw away the peel. Simply place it around the plants where the cats have been digging and they should do it no more. Cats don't like the smell of the oil from orange peel (limonene).

Go old style

Would you like to taste good old fashioned vegetable and fruit varieties? Then source what are called heritage seeds or heirloom seeds and discover a new world of tastes and some great old fashioned names. For example, Sheep's Nose, Greasy Jack, Eggleton Styre and Grand Duke Constantine are all names of great tasting traditional apples.

Weed it out

I remember being told as a kid that a weed was just a flower in the wrong place. So if you get a flower growing in the wrong place, don't reach for the weed killer, try one of these alternatives:

- Boiling water can be poured over a weed, which will then shrivel and die.

- White vinegar poured straight onto the weed will also kill it. But remember to treat just the weed and not the area around as the vinegar will also kill other plants.

- Eat them! That's right, some weeds are edible. Why waste time killing them when you can put them on the plate and enjoy. However, check and double check that they're safe before you have a nibble!

GREEN FACT

The oldest known apple tree was sown during the year of 1810 and is a Bramley's Seedling, it is still growing and producing apples in Southwell, Nottinghamshire, England. The oldest known pear tree is almost 400 years old. It was planted by the first governor of Massachusetts, John Endicott, hence being known as The Endicott Pear Tree. Evidence suggests that it was shipped from England on the ship Arbella in 1630 and was planted sometime during 1632.

Yesterday's news

If you have flower beds, try keep the moisture in by adding a top layer. This could be compost, tree bark or even yesterday's newspapers. This will not only benefit your plants but will also cut down on the amount you have to water them during dry periods.

Composting – getting it right:

If you just throw everything on a pile, nature will still work her wonders; however, try these tips to speed the process:

- Try to keep a good balance between dry stuff (newspapers, straw) and wet stuff (kitchen scraps, grass cuttings). Too dry and it'll take years. Too wet and it'll start to smell.

- Allow grass clippings to dry slightly before adding.

- When starting a new compost pile, pick a place that has well drained soil and break up the surface of the soil to help the worms move in. Don't put it in a place where it will be in the sun all day as this may dry it out too much.

- To check your compost is warm (which is when the magic happens), dig a small hole, place your hand near this hole and if it feels warm you're okay. If it's cold, you can help by adding green vegetation or fresh manure.

- Don't have huge lumps of things; break them down into smaller lumps to help the process.

- If your compost is not contained but simply a pile hidden in the corner of the garden, speed the process up by turning over regularly. Just be aware that something may have moved in so take great care where you stab that fork.

- Stuff you can add includes tea leaves, uncooked vegetables, eggshells, cardboard, newspapers, leaves and grass, and manure from rabbits/horses.

- Things you should never add include droppings from dogs and cats.

Make your own

Let your garden benefit from making your own compost. There are a number of ways of doing this. One way is to have your own wormery (see the tip in the pet section), another is to put your bin on a diet and place all your kitchen waste in a composter.

Dandelion treat

Now, did you know that all parts of the dandelion are edible? The root can be boiled or used in a stir-fry just like other root vegetables. The flower can be boiled and used as a part of a stir-fry or why not try turning it into dandelion wine? The leaves can be boiled, just like spinach, or washed and used as part of a green salad. If you want some ideas on how versatile this weed is then search on the internet for dandelion recipes and you'll be spoilt for choice.

GREEN FACT

Did you know that it's estimated that 30% of all food consumed by humans was directly or indirectly pollinated by bees? Also, to date, 1.5 million types of life form have been described and documented and 1 million of these were insects!

Alternative to fertilizer

Rather than using a bag of fertilizer, why not use those coffee grinds or cold coffee (black obviously). Simply sprinkle the ground near your plants and dig them in. Alternatively, allow the coffee to go cold and you have a liquid fertilizer ready and waiting. Or, if you have some beer left over from the previous night (unlikely I know, but it does happen sometimes) then use that as a liquid fertilizer as well. Cold tea or broken open tea bags are also a great feed for lime-hating plants, such as rhododendrons and camellias.

Lifestyle

> **66** If all the beasts were gone, men would die from a great loneliness of spirit, for whatever happens to the beasts also happens to the man. All things are connected. Whatever befalls the Earth befalls the sons of the Earth. **99**

Chief Seattle (1786-1866)

Chapter 3
Lifestyle

In almost everything we do we can lessen the effect we have on the environment. If it's just making something last a little longer than we would normally, to thinking about where we make our purchases, it all has a knock on effect. We often forget that companies are not in control of our purses or wallets and it is us who decide where our money goes. So if a company does not share the same views you do, then don't purchase their products. Once they get the message that they don't stock, sell or make what you want, they'll have to change their ways in order to stay in business. So choose a lifestyle that mirrors your beliefs and 'drag' the rest of the world with you, kicking and screaming if you have to!

Holy order

We all know we should walk more, use buses more or even ride a bike. But let's face it, we humans are lazy. So the car has become a necessary evil for most of us. But you can cut down the amount of damage you do by putting your racing helmet away and start driving like a nun! Driving with less pressure on the accelerator will decrease fuel consumption and the emissions your car creates. There is even a device called 'Magno Fuel' which, through the wonders of science, reportedly reduces your fuel usage by up to 15%.

Buy recycled

Today, there are a huge number of items made from recycled materials. Paper is the one that springs to mind, from kitchen rolls to toilet tissues. But you can go one step further and buy items that started life as something else. For example, drinks glasses that were once bottles and pencil cases that were once tires.

GREEN FACT

Bottled water has a carbon footprint of 6½oz (185g) on average; this includes the making of the bottle, filling the bottle, shipping, and you getting it home. However, water from the tap is just 0.01oz (0.3g).

Car-tastrophe

Many of us only give the welfare of our car a second thought when it needs an annual safety and emissions inspection (M.O.T.) or when it won't start. However, by keeping your car tuned, with your tires at the correct pressure, you can minimize your fuel consumption and cut down on emissions. For example, did you know that by keeping your tires at the right pressure you can reduce the amount of fuel you use by around 5 to 10%? Lastly, if you keep your car uncluttered you can decrease your fuel usage.

That carbon footprint

A few years ago, no-one knew what a carbon footprint was let alone worried about it. Unfortunately, our modern lives mean we all leave a footprint but there are ways we can help offset it. Place 'offsetting carbon foot print' in your chosen search engine and you'll discover a whole range of sites that allow you to invest in planting trees, providing help to developing nations, investing in renewable energy. Although, this is not the answer but it all helps.

Toy land

Every year, thousands and thousands of new toys are produced, given, played with and then left unloved. The change in status is because they break, the batteries run out or they are not 'loved' any more. Rather than consign them to the bin, toys that are still working can be donated either to a local charity, local toy library, hospice or hospital. If you don't have a local toy library but you have a child who is a member of a school or club, then why not start a swap box? Get everyone to put in a toy to start the ball rolling. Then, in order to take a toy, one must be put in. Once they are fed up with this toy they simply take it back and swap it for another one.

GREEN FACT
Did you know that polystyrene cups can take up to 100 years to degrade whilst other commonly used plastics can take up to 450 years?

Power to the people

Each year huge numbers of batteries are thrown away and these little devils become time bombs in our landfill sites. There are alternatives. The first is obvious; don't buy something that needs batteries. If you do have an item that is battery operated then invest in rechargeable batteries. They obviously have a longer life and, if used correctly, can be reused time and time again.

It's a wind up

Following on from the tip above, next time you have to renew a torch, radio, clock or even your MP3 player, why not get a wind up version. They are now just as competitive price wise with battery guzzlers and are cheaper to run.

"We have beautiful beaches, if people could just think about what they flush down the toilet... "

Gill Bell, Marine Conservation Society

Heat retention

When the cold nights draw in, resist turning up the thermostat; go and put on an extra layer! Also, try drawing the curtains at dusk to stop the heat from escaping via the windows. This will cut down on draughts and reduce your fuel bills.

Home laundry

When the rain is beating against your windows, try resisting the urge to put that washing over a radiator to dry. This does dry your clothes; unfortunately, it also lowers the temperature of the room. The damp clothes fool the radiator into thinking it must work harder, which pushes up those fuel bills in turn. Try investing in an old fashioned clothes horse. I know you can't rely on the weather, however, I use my sun shade as an aid to drying. I simply put my washing under it when it's warm enough for the clothes to dry but the rain is still falling from the heavens.

Travel sickness

Unfortunately, the modern way of life dictates that many of us rely heavily on our cars. To get to and from work, take the kids to their various after school activities, to get the shopping, etc. There are ways to cut down on their use. Think about the trip you are making. Can you car share? Can you double up on tasks? For example, if you are passing today somewhere you'll have to drop off something tomorrow, then drop it off today. It just needs a little planning. I know it sounds a drag but it can be done. A few years ago we had a fuel strike. Knowing I wouldn't be able to fill my car, I changed my habits and made the fuel last around 50% longer.

Mobile madness

How often have you changed your phone just because it looks a little old or because you no longer like its shape? A cell phone is a tool, not a fashion accessory. I recently had to change my phone and was feeling pleased with myself because I'd made it last six years, then my mum beat me. She'd made hers last eight! Also, don't just throw away those phones. Many charities can turn those phones into cash, by recycling.

Time to replace

If an item breaks down, see if you can get it mended first. If you can't and you have to replace it, keep an eye out for labeling schemes that identify energy-efficient products. Look for the Energy Saving Recommended logo, which shows you how efficiently or not the item uses energy. Typically, the better designed a produce is with regards to energy consumption the higher their price, however, if cared for over its life, this will be recouped through reduced fuel bills.

Spiderman and Dangermouse

Rather than killing everything that comes into the house, try catching it first. Try the old trick of using a glass and piece of card with spiders. However, if you can't build up the courage do to this then try **www. spidercatcher.net**. If you are having problems with something a little bigger, then try using a humane trap. When using these, remember you MUST check everyday and, when releasing back into the wild, you'll need to go for a little walk and release away from other homes.

GREEN FACT
On average, the life span of a cell phone is just 18 months.

It's a gift

Next time you give a present, do you really have to wrap it in a brand new piece of wrapping paper? What about giving the gift in a gift bag that can be used again and again? Or try wrapping the gift in a scrap of fun fabric or simply tying the bag the gift came in with a piece of ribbon. Get creative; you'll be surprised with what you come up with.

> **66** We do not inherit the earth from our ancestors; we borrow it from our children. **99**

Native American Proverb

Go antique

It's that time of year when you need to rush out and buy a gift for a loved one. Oh what to get? Perhaps one question you should ask yourself is does it have to be brand new? What about popping along to the local antique shop to see if you can pick up something a little different?

Become involved

We all have busy lives but get involved with local environmental issues. Even if it's just one hour a week. You will not only be helping others and the environment but you may also find you enjoy it! If you visit your local library, they often have leaflets about local organizations looking for help. Alternatively, type 'local charities' or 'local environmental organizations' into your chosen search engine to find something local to you. If getting dirty by planting trees is not your thing, many also need office staff and the great thing is that now much of this can be done remotely so you don't even have to leave home to help.

Don't drop it

Each year, large quantities of little bits of rubbish are dropped. It seems obvious to say but this not only looks unsightly, it can cause problems for our wildlife. So don't drop it, keep it in your pocket and take it home. In April 2009, it was estimated, there are now 46,000 pieces of plastic per square kilometer of the world's oceans, killing a million seabirds and 100,000 marine mammals each year. Not all of this has been directly dropped into the oceans but has been blown from our land masses and taken out to sea by our rivers.

GREEN FACT

It is estimated that 150 billion plastic bags are used worldwide each year, which causes untold havoc on our environment and our wildlife!

The power of the pen

If a company or event annoys you then write to the people who can do something about it. For example, there was a certain fast food restaurant that sold ice-cream in a tub. All very well for us, it was handy and made eating the ice-cream easier, no drips down the side. However, the opening of the lid was just the right size for animals to get their head stuck, they then suffered a long and lingering death by starvation. It may have taken a few years and many, many letters of complaint, but this certain large fast food chain relented and redesigned the containers. People power can work!

The 3 'R's

Reduce, reuse and recycle. Simply put, try to reduce what you use in everyday life, reuse what you can when you can, and recycle as much as you can. For a little help with this, there is a marvelous little book called Reduce, Reuse, Recycle by Nicky Scott, which is an A-Z of the 3 Rs. It covers everything from Aerosols to Zero waste.

Go retro

Each year, we buy new clothes that are the latest fashion, however, wearing vintage clothing is also the latest fashion. It allows you to be a little different, to make a statement, often save money, and allows you to be a little greener along the way. A few years ago I taught a student who never bought new clothes and she always looked fantastic. She would buy designer labels at a fraction of the cost and, if it didn't fit her, it was adapted, altered and chopped up to become something else.

Swap shop

If you're of the right age (and lived in the UK) you'll remember the Saturday show Swap Shop, which allowed kids to swap items for others, along with all the other mayhem that went on during the show. Today there are equivalents to this. In the UK they are known as LETS (Local Exchange

Trading Schemes). They are local networks where people can exchange any type of goods or services for something else. If you have a skill, you can earn yourself 'credits' that can then be traded for another skill. So do a little research and see if you have one of these that covers your local area and get swapping.

Nothing's free

There are ways in which you can give to charity and also get something back. When it comes to giving a card, buy one where some of the money goes towards a charity, or take out a credit card where some of the spending power you wield goes towards a charity. Some banks offer this as a service, however, many of the larger charity organizations also offer their own.

GREEN FACT

Every year, the average bin contains enough unrealized energy to:

- Heat enough water for 500 baths
- Heat enough water for 3,500 showers
- Run a television for 5,000 hours

Going veggie

A cow produces 15lbs (6.8kg) of global warming gas (methane) in its life. So cutting down on your meat intake can help reduce these omissions. However, as with everything, there are choices that have to be made. For example, many products like tofu or textured vegetable protein are made from soya beans and most of the soya beans grown worldwide are genetically modified, and it's still hotly debated on how green this is. So if you're buying products that are suitable for veggies, you still have to read the label.

66 There is a sufficiency in the world for man's need but not for man's greed. 99

Mahatma Gandhi

Become an entrepreneur

Rather than have a house full of clutter, why not become an entrepreneur and use one of the many auction sites to sell those items you no longer need? If the urge takes you, why not donate the money raised to a charity of your choice? These auction sites have made selling easy, fun and (be warned) very addictive.

Re-gifting

Some see this as rude, giving away a gift you've received to someone else. But if they're true friends they'll understand that this is your way of being green. Re-gifting means you're reducing the need to buy new, reusing something that would otherwise sit unloved or perhaps even end up taking up valuable space in landfill sites.

Aim for zero waste

Aim for zero waste and put your bin on a diet. Reduce the goods you buy, recycle where you can, compost, repair, reuse; throw nothing away. Get the kids crafting using any cardboard you have. It'll save you money and you may even find you enjoy the task of 'thinking out of the box!' Other ways to cut down on your waste include:

- Use a lunch box for your packed lunch rather than foil.

- Buy durable products rather than 'use once' items.

- Buy loose fruit and vegetables and if the items you buy are over-packed, leave the packaging at the shop, so they get the idea!

- Buy large packets and bottles rather than lots of small ones.

- Buy concentrated products and refill bottles where you can.

No more mail

Junk mail is not only annoying but it also wastes precious resources. So if you don't want to know about the latest gadget, the biggest gym, or car insurance for the third time in a year, then take yourself off mail listings. Also, next time you fill out any form, remember to put that tick in the little box they hide at the end, stating you don't want mailings. Or why not produce a small poster and stick it in your window stating you don't want leaflets pushed through your door.

GREEN FACT

Did you know that it takes between 12 – 15 years for the butt of a cigarette to breakdown? Filters collect chemicals like cadmium, lead and arsenic. These chemicals can leach into water and just one cigarette filter is toxic enough to kill water fleas in 14 pints (eight liters) of water (K. Register, 2000). Butts have also been found in the guts of whales, dolphins, sea birds, fish, and turtles. The toxins these butts release can cause inflammation of the animal's digestive system and occasionally even cause death. In an annual global survey of litter, cigarette butts have been the number one item found for 17 years running. In September 2006, over 1.9 million cigarette butts were recorded from beaches around the world (Ocean Conservancy, 2007).

Green party

Next time you have friends round, try to host a green party. For large gatherings, rather than using plastic knives, forks and cups, source corn plastic or sugarcane plastic items, which are biodegradable. For cups why not rent glasses instead? Rather than balloons for decorations why not get the kids to make alternatives from recycled materials, these are sure to become a talking point during the party. For smaller gatherings, rather than use paper napkins invest in cloth napkins that can be used again and again.

Babies and Children

66 It is the sweet, simple things of life which are the real ones after all. **99**

Laura Ingalls Wilder

Chapter 4
Babies and Children

There are many versions of the following quote: "give me the child, and I will mold the man." But they all mean the same basic thing. Which is whatever you teach a child will be with them for life. So what better way to safeguard the environment and our planet than to instill love and respect for the world around us early in a child's life?

Baby shower

When planning your baby shower provide suggestions for what you'd like. Ask family and friends not to 'shower' you with gifts you don't really need. You could request simply hard cash, which could be the start of that college fund. Perhaps ask for an item that is created using environmentally friendly materials. Even ask for home made vouchers, where the giver offers their future services, baby sitting for example.

Green fingers

One of the best ways to get children interested in the environment is to introduce them to joys of the world around them. If you are lucky enough to have a garden, then perhaps grow wild flowers from seed, or plant a small tree and watch it grow. Create bug homes and place them around the garden and watch the bird population grow as their food source increases. If you don't have a garden, perhaps try obtaining an allotment and grow anything from sun flowers (a great source of food for the birds) to vegetables for yourselves.

Happy Nappy's or Dappy Diapers

We all realize that, in an ideal world, you would not have to make a choice between the convenience of the disposable nappy/diaper and the old fashioned clothe version. However, sometimes life forces us to make decisions we are not 100% happy with. So why not try to use the clothe version whenever possible. Research and use a local nappy/diaper cleaning service that is both convenient and environmentally friendly. Then use a chlorine-free disposable one for those times when you are out and about and have no-where to store the soiled item. If you can cut down on the number of disposables you use by just 50%, that will make a huge difference.

GREEN FACT

It is estimated that 49 – 60 million nappies/diapers in the US are thrown away each and every day of the year. These end up in landfill and it's estimated that the plastic sections take anywhere between 200 to 500 years to decompose! Each baby will use approximately 5,300 disposable nappies/diapers from birth to that glorious moment when they are toilet trained. It takes an amazing 440 – 880 lbs (200kg – 400kg) of fluff pulp and 286 lbs (82kg) of plastic (including packaging) per year to supply a single baby with disposables.

Interior design

When creating a new room for the new arrival or perhaps updating an existing bedroom, you don't have to lavish out on new furniture. Why not take a trip to the local auction house and purchase something a little different. You'll not only save yourself some money but may even obtain a piece of furniture that will be handed down from one generation to the next.

Cut of your cloth

There is a temptation when a new baby comes along, to buy it a whole wardrobe of new clothes. Why go to the expense? Enjoy the fact that a baby will wear anything you put it in without question (unlike those wonderful tweenage and teenage years you have to look forward to) and dress them in hand-me-downs or clothes purchased from thrift/charity shops, etc.

The three R's

Children learn from us. So as you recycle, reuse and reduce, explain why you are doing this to them. Make it fun; make it a game and they'll not see these activities as a chore.

Get involved

Why not encourage the children to become involved in local 'green' activities? If you live near the beach, why not contact local groups who organize beach cleans and ask if you can help. Perhaps suggest to their school that the children create an area for wildlife. This can be linked to their studies in school and the school will benefit from a new 'outdoor' classroom. Perhaps contact a local charity or non-profit organization and ask if there is something you can do to help as a family. It could be anything from raising awareness to organizing a fund raising event.

Little entrepreneur

Why not encourage the children to scour their bedrooms and the house for toys, books, clothes they no longer use and hold a garage sale or similar. It'll not only help you reduce the amount of clutter in the house but will also begin to teach them the importance of not throwing unwanted items away and also of earning money.

Piggy bank

Unfortunately, we all need to understand the importance of money and the effects that it can have on the world around us. Rather than having just one piggy bank, why not have a couple? Each one is allocated a different use. The first could be for day trips to local places of interest, which could include places like stables for rescued horses, etc. The second could be money they will donate to good causes. This will hopefully teach them the joys of giving, what a difference their money can make and to encourage them to be compassionate. Also tell them that you will match any donation they make and they can choose the organization the donation goes to.

As soft as a babies bottom

Unless your child is suffering from a rash, why spend all your money on needless potions and lotions? If their skin does not need help to repair or needs protection (for example, sun block) why cover them in something they don't need. It'll be healthier for them and better for the environment if you keep the use of these items to a minimum. If you find you have to use them perhaps find skin care products that use natural ingredients.

Kick the habit

We all know we shouldn't smoke whilst children are around. So why not take the opportunity to kick the habit, rather than subject yourself to standing outside sneaking 'a crafty one' in all weathers. Also think of all the money you'll be saving. You could put it towards a great family day out.

Toy story

A US government funded study into the number of toys a child has concluded that too many toys can restrict a child's development. "They get overwhelmed and over-stimulated and cannot concentrate on any one thing long enough to learn from it, so they just shut down. Too many toys mean they are not learning to play imaginatively either." (Claire Lerner, child-development worker). Also, a study by the University of Stirling recently concluded that expensive, hi-tech toys are a waste of money. Children learn just as much from playing with traditional toys. So next time you're at a local fair, keep an eye out for a wood worker and see if you can source those traditional wooden toys many of us grew up with.

" Humankind has not woven
the web of life.
    We are but one thread within it.
Whatever we do to the web,
    We do to ourselves.
All things are bound together.
    All things connect. "

Chief Seattle, 1855

Back To School

When children return to school, it appears they need more and more 'stuff'. Rather than buying all those items unnecessarily, what follows are a few ideas that will make going back to school greener:

From last term

Check what they have left over from last term before you go and buy anything new. Create a list of what you need. Pads that are half full can be utilized. Simply remove the unused pages and bind them together to create a new pad. Old wall paper, brown paper, saved wrapping paper, etc. can be used to create a new cover. Let the children get creative and have fun so they don't feel they are missing out by reusing old pads.

Pens, pencils and cases

If you discover that pens and pencils are needed then invest in pencils that are made from recycled materials, such as old tires. A variety of pens also made from recycled materials can be sourced, including biros that are bio-degradable. If they need pencil cases, why not have a go at making your own from a pair of old jeans. Alternatively, purchase a pencil case that is created from an old tire.

Lunch time

Instead of using plastic lunch bags, invest in a lunch box that can be used again and again. At the end of the day they can be washed and are ready for use the next morning. Place 'eco lunch box' into your chosen search engine and you'll be amazed at the range now available.

Keep them hydrated

Instead of sending them off with pre-bottled water, invest in a good quality water bottle that can be filled each morning. The added bonus is that this bottle can be used during the holiday period on day trips, etc.

Swap Shop

Why not set up a clothes and toy swap shop with other local families. When your child grows out of their clothes or becomes bored with a toy, simply put the clothes or toys in and take something 'new' out. It'll save you money and means you'll not be purchasing new items that use precious resources.

Trash into art

Rather than throw away those old egg cartons, why not turn them into art? Turn boxes into games and old greetings cards into new ones. The Internet is a great resource for this and is brimming with simple to copy ideas.

Family friends

If you are lucky enough to have a park near by, why not introduce the children to some of the creatures that live there. If there is a pond with wild fowl, why not take food with you. However, resist the temptation to take bread, as this is an unsuitable food for most wild fowl. Encourage the children to research what is suitable food.

Keeping healthy

We all know that, by keeping healthy, we not only are able to enjoy life more but we also reduce our need for medical treatment, which in turn reduces the amount of medication we use. This is not only good for us but also for the environment. So rather than jump in the car to go to school, why not walk or take the bike. Perhaps team up with other families in the area and create a 'walking bus.'

Turn detective

When you go shopping, encourage the children to read the labels. What's in the food you are buying? Where did it come from? Was it produced locally? Is it a fair-trade product? They'll enjoy being involved and it will encourage them to think about issues such as the 'food miles' and how it was produced.

Halloween fun

Each and every year thousands are spent on this one holiday alone. The costs to you and the environment can be kept to a minimum if you think outside the box and prepare for the big night a week or so before hand. Also, getting the children involved with this preparation will increase their enjoyment. So what follows are a few tips just for Halloween.

Costumes:

Rather than purchase or hire a costume, have a go at making one yourself. With a little imagination and some fake blood many an unwanted garment can be changed into a ghostly garment. If you are stuck for ideas, place 'halloween costume ideas for children' in your chosen search engine and you'll be rewarded with a host of great ideas.

Trick or Treat bag:

Turn an old pillow case into a trick or treat bag. With the addition of a scary face drawn on the front using pens, it'll serve just as well as any shop purchased bag. Or cover a basket in scraps of red fabric for something a little different.

Peter Pumpkin:

If you carve out a pumpkin, instead of throwing away the flesh and the pips use them to create tasty treats you can give out on the night. Again, the web is a great source for recipes.

Other treats:

Rather than purchase sweets that are over packaged, why not make your own? Apples dipped in chocolate are both a tasty and healthier option. Perhaps make your own fudge and put it into small bags tied with strips of fabric from an old T-shirt (red of course). The children will love making them and giving them out when their friends knock on the door.

Turn off the toons

Although we all know we should watch less TV, most of us realize that the pull of the TV is great on many children. So rather than fight it, why not use it to your advantage. Turn off those toons and get them watching the Discovery For Kids channel or something similar. In this way, they grow up knowing about the world, how fragile it is and what we can all do to help.

Liners and wipes

Did you know that wipes and liners can include propylene glycol (which is a binder found in antifreeze), as well as parabens (compounds commonly used as preservatives) and perfume (which can contain up to 600 different chemicals). So try to steer clear of these and use organic cotton wool and water instead.

What's on your doorstep?

Take the children for a walk with pencils, paper and camera in hand. Encourage them to write about what they see and to take photographs.

When they get home they can use this to keep an eco-journal. Places can be visited during different times of the year. Children will get to see exactly how the seasons effects the world in which they live and the impact we have.

Little chefs

Encourage the children to explore the joys of cooking. It will not only cut down on the consumption of junk food but will also give them an understanding of where their food comes from. This could be tied in with a trip to the local farmers market so they can learn to cook with seasonal produce that has been grown locally.

Moving on

Although it is entirely down to the individual, babies normally start to eat solid food when they are about six months old. Although shop purchased food in a jar is convenient, they have a large carbon foot print. So why not have a go at creating your own pureed baby food. For convenience, create batches and place them in suitable sterilized containers, freeze, and then take out when needed. There are a great number of books available containing recipes that will meet your baby's dietary requirements.

Shoes off

We all know how much children crawl or play on the floor when at home. So reduce the amount of dirt and dust by encouraging the entire family to get into the habit of taking off their shoes as soon as they come in.

Celebration time

Encourage the children to discover our environment and the different people of this fantastically complex world by celebrating a different day each month. It's not only fun but will also broaden their minds. To start you off, here are a few suggestions:

Jan	1st	Global Family Day, World Day of Peace
Feb	12th	Darwin Day
Feb	22nd	International Scouts Day and World Thinking Day
Mar	14th	International Day of Action for Rivers
Mar	22nd	World Day of Water
Apr	21st	World Creativity and Innovation Day
Apr	22nd	Earth Day
May	Second Sat	World Fair Trade Day
May	23rd	World Turtle Day
Jun	5th	World Environment Day
Jun	8th	World Ocean Day
Jul	11th	World Population Day
Jul	16th	World Snake Day
Aug	9th	International Day of the World's Indigenous People
Aug	Last Sun	International Friendship Day
Sep	21st	World Gratitude Day
Sep	22nd	World Car-free Day
Oct	First Mon	World Habitat Day
Oct	4th	World Animal Day
Nov	13th	World Kindness Day
Nov	21st	World Hello Day
Dec	1st	World Aids Day
Dec	11th	International Mountain Day

Please note all dates were correct at the time of going to print.

On Holiday

66 There are no passengers on Spaceship Earth. We are all crew. **99**

Marshall McLuhan

Chapter 5
On holiday

Today, our holidays not only allow us to recharge our batteries but they are increasingly used as a statement of our position and how much we have managed to 'squirrel' away in the bank. We seem to think we must travel half the globe in order to discover something new and exciting. But we don't have to spend hours cramped in tight seats, next to someone we've never met before, to have a great holiday. Read on and find ways to have a great green holiday.

Helping hand

Try a holiday with a difference and give your time to something or someone who will really benefit. Check out:

www.responsiblevacation.com – US readers

www.responsibletravel.com – UK readers

They offer holidays that give you the opportunity to teach English in African countries, conserve the beaches where turtles nest, or work in an animal rescue center.

Take it with you

If you decided to stay in a hotel, then take your own toiletries with you and try to avoid those little 'free' bottles of shampoo, conditioner and shower gel. Those little bottles not only waste plastic but how often do you only use half the bottle, meaning the other half ends up in the bin?

" Take nothing but pictures. Leave nothing but footprints. Kill nothing but time. **"**

Motto of the Baltimore Grotto Caving Society

Research

Before you go, do a little research into where you're going and if you book via a large holiday company, check their green credentials. Do they use local people as reps? Do they invest in the local economy? If you don't like the answers then let the company know why you'll not be using their services. Hitting their pocket is a sure way to 'convert' them! If you want to discover if the place where you are staying is really committed, then check out: **www.ec3global.com.** If you want to ensure where you are staying benefits the local community, then get hold of The Ethical Travel Guide which lists over 300 places to visit and stay in 60 countries and have a positive impact on local people and their environment. Also check out: **www.iknowagreatplace.com** which allows you to ask questions and covers great places worldwide.

All in

Try not to go for one of those all inclusive holidays. Very little, if any, of the money generated by your stay will make it out into the local community. Unless their ethical statement states they support the local community. So before you book don't be afraid to ask questions.

GREEN FACT

Over a short flight (approximately 311 miles or 500km) an aeroplane produces around three times more CO_2 than a train.

The Countryside Code

When out and about enjoying the local scenery and wildlife, think Countryside Code. The basics are:

- Take nothing but photographs.

- Leave nothing, even footprints, if you can help it!

- Ensure you close all gates.

- Stick to marked paths, so you don't destroy plant and animal life.

- Keep dogs (and over excited children) under control.

- Clean up after your pooch.

Helping the hotels

When staying in a hotel, there are ways you can help them become greener; these include:

- Say no to new towels and sheets everyday.

- Turn off everything when you leave your room.

- Reduce paper by checking out via the hotel's electronic check-out system.

- Ask for drinking glasses and don't use plastic cups.

- Give them feedback when you leave, providing them with a few hints and tips on becoming greener.

Alternative accommodation

Once you've found the ideal place for your holiday, don't automatically think hotel. Why not contact the local tourist information and ask about small family run hotels, B & Bs, static caravan sites or cottages? Many of these will be owned by local people who will spend the money they earn from you locally. You'll be supporting the local economy twice over. Also, if you go self-catering, you'll find it easier to keep your green values whilst away.

Drink and think

Get organized and when going out for the day take a drink with you so you don't end up purchasing a bottle of water. Just think of all that money you'll be saving, which can then be used to buy something more interesting.

Watching the locals

Holidays are a great time to discover the local wildlife. But, when booking that wildlife excursion, check that the organizer is aware of and takes into account the needs of the wildlife first. If you don't like what you find then contact a local conservation charity, many of whom run trips where you know they'll put the wildlife first. It's also a great way of helping them look after what you are going to see.

Light, not so fantastic

Pollution is not just waste and fumes, it's also light and noise. For example, it may be lovely to sit in a bar enjoying a cooled drink listening to the waves but if it's turtle hatching time then those little turtles could get confused and head towards the bar rather than to the sea. If you come across such a bar that doesn't seem to care what havoc its lights are causing, tell them you'll not be drinking there and give them this website address:

http://myfwc.com/research/

From here an article can be downloaded, giving suggestions on what simple steps can be taken to reduce the impact of lighting. Then, once they've followed its tips, they can install a sign outside telling everyone just how good they are!

Noisy neighbors

We humans are noisy creatures as we insist on climbing aboard jet skis and the like. In studies, it's been found that 'long term exposure to noise can cause excessive stimulation to the nervous system and chronic stress that is harmful to the health of wildlife species and their reproductive fitness' (Fletcher, 1980; 1990). Also, many 'animals rely on their hearing to avoid predators, obtain food, and communicate… studies have documented hearing loss caused from motorcycle noise in the desert iguana (Bondello, 1976) and the kangaroo rat, an endangered species' (Bondello and

Brattstrom, 1979). So before you have a go at that dune buggy, talk to the operators to find out what precautions they take.

Buy local

When buying the obligatory presents, look for local suppliers and buy local produce. I can remember a number of years ago we took a long weekend break on the Norfolk coast (UK) and stumbled across a local brewery. Needless to say we invested in a few bottles and managed to enjoy our holiday memories each time we opened another bottle of their lovely product. However, do be careful what you buy; for example, don't purchase items made from hardwoods, corals, shells, ivory or fur.

GREEN FACT

Did you know the word tourism comes from the Hebrew word 'tora' which means study, learn, or search?

Come fly with me

If you have no alternative to flying then organize your tickets electronically. It saves paper and you'll be less likely to lose your documents when you are traveling.

Pedal power

If you're staying somewhere where it would be safe to use pedal power then why not give it a go? It's fun, it gives you the opportunity to really see your environment, you get the chance to meet the locals, and it's good for your fitness levels. If staying in a hotel, ask the concierge if they know of a local rental place, or try the local tourist information. Alternatively, if you're able to, why not take your own bike?

"" I conceive that the land belongs to a vast family of which many are dead, few are living, and countless numbers are still unborn. ""

A Chieftain from Nigeria

Brochure bonkers

How often have you popped into a local travel agent and come out with armfuls of brochures only to find they repeat the same information time and time again? Much of, if not all, the information you can find in these brochures can be found online. So save yourself the trip and yet more paper to recycle by letting your fingers do the research.

On your way out

Just before you close the door and say goodbye to your castle for those two weeks you'll be away, remember to go round each and every room to check all the plugs. Turn off or, even better, ensure plugs have been pulled out. They consume energy even on standby, you'll also cut down on the possibility of fires when you're away.

It's in the planning

When you begin to plan your holiday try to also plan the route you'll take to get there. Try to use train or public transport where possible. If you have to fly, try to fly direct, which cuts down on those nasty internal flights. Once there, if you can't walk or cycle to a place of interest, then check out local bus companies and make the ride part of the adventure. If you're unsure about traveling using these methods, then check out this site: **www.seat61.com** which is full of useful information.

GREEN FACT

It is estimated that tourism employs around 231 million people, and generates 8 – 10% of the world's total GDP.

Go solar

When we travel, we seem to insist on taking all those little gadgets we can't do without: phones, iPods and electronic games. All of which need charging. Rather than finding the nearest plug socket, why not invest in a solar charger? Many come with adaptors enabling you to charge a whole range of items.

Too many feet

When I was at University, we studied what I think was called 'the honey pot effect' (I could be wrong on the name, it's a long time ago) but I do remember the gist of what the effect was. Basically, we all want to go to see the same places, like a bee around a honey pot. This obviously has an affect on the environment and the wildlife we want to see. Thus, we are actually destroying what we went to see in the first place. So resist following the swarm and visit something a little out of the way. This will not only lessen the impact but will also share out the income generated by tourists, rather than just one place earning the lion's share.

Grow organic

If you would love to have a holiday that's a little bit different then why not have a 'holiday' on an organic farm or smallholding? A little research is sure to come up with some suggestions for you.

Photos with the locals

Whilst on holiday, it may be tempting to have your photograph taken with that cute animal by a beach photographer. However, consider where that animal came from (many chimps, for example, are caught as babies in the wild, their mothers killed in the process) and its fate once it's not so cute.

Snow way!

If you prefer a little snow rather than sun then try to ensure your activities have as little impact as possible on the local environment. Check out **www.skiclub.co.uk,** which states their aim is 'to seek to improve the environmental performance of the Club and its members in a way that helps safeguard the natural environment and the long-term future of skiing.' Although a UK based site, it has loads of info that can be used by skiers worldwide.

All in one

Rather than have a long weekend here and another there, save the time and the money and have one big holiday. That'll give you the opportunity to be able to spend a little more time traveling, so you can make the journey via boat, train or bus to become part of the holiday experience.

Wish you were here

Rather than sending postcards, why not email your friends a lovely photograph you've taken yourself? Much more personal! Or send a text with a picture attached.

Chill out

It has been estimated that, if just half of us staying in a hotel room with air-conditioning were to turn it off whilst out of the room during one week, we could reduce CO_2 emissions by 5 million tonnes.

Something a little different

Rather than go for a boring old cruise, think out of the box. Believe it or not you can travel by cargo ship; they often go to places you'd not normally travel to via conventional liners. A growing number of companies help you find a cargo ship going to your destination and will also help you book the passage. Either put 'travel by cargo ship' in any of the search engines or check out **www.travltips.com** or **www.freighterworld.com**.

Water wings

Rather than ride that jet ski or get pulled into the air suspended from a large kite behind a motor boat, there are lots of other ways to enjoy a dip and not create a huge wave. Try canoeing, rafting, sailing, rowing or even snorkeling, swimming or diving.

Yester-year

Rediscover the holidays from your childhood, where you pitched up a tent and simply went walking. The Camping and Caravanning Club in the UK (www.campingandcaravanningclub.co.uk) gives an award called The David Bellamy Conservation Award, which ensures holiday, caravan, camping, and residential parks really do follow green ethics, including:

- Cultivating local flora and fauna.

- Creating habitats to encourage wildlife.

- Having good recycling/waste management.

- Having good community links for produce/materials.

For camping in other parts of the world, research your local camping organization.

GREEN FACT
Did you know that if you brush against coral whilst swimming it'll take 25 years to recover?

Bug off

Rather than using nasty chemicals to keep the bugs at bay, try citronella, eucalyptus, mint or clove. If you want to have a go at making your own, type 'insect repellent' in your chosen search engine and a whole array of alternatives will pop up. One solution is to take garlic tablets once a day two weeks before you go away.

Going solar

There are a growing number of camping related items that use solar power. For example, you can now purchase tents that store the power of the sun during the day whilst you are out and provide you with free lighting and heat on your return. Other items available also include a solar powered hat with built-in light.

“ I believe in God, only I spell it Nature. **”**

Frank Lloyd Wright, Architect and Interior Designer (1867-1959)

When you're home

Whilst away, you may have come across a charity or project that still needs your help when you get home. Why not support them once a month with a small donation? Many tour operators support a number of charities, so you could ask them while you're there. On your return journey you could put your holiday currency in the paper envelope given out on your flight. However, here is a list of some charities you may wish to help:

- www.bornfree.org.uk

An international wildlife charity working to stop individual wild animals suffering and protecting threatened species in the wild.

- www.foc-uk.com

Help prevent wildlife & habitat degradation in the Masai Mara.

- www.ifaw.org/

The International Fund for Animal Welfare saves animals in crisis from around the world.

- www.thebrooke.org

Provides care to working horses around the world, so the people who rely on them can support themselves and their families.

- www.birdlife.org

BirdLife International is an international conservation organization working to protect the world's birds and their natural habitats.

- www.foe.co.uk

Friends of the Earth is an international network of environmental organizations in 70 countries.

- www.wetlands.org

Wetlands International is a global non-profit organization dedicated solely to the work of wetland conservation and sustainable management.

- www.wwf.org.uk

The World Wide Fund for Nature is an international nongovernmental organization working for the conservation, research, and restoration of the natural environment.

This is obviously just the tip of the iceberg when it comes to good causes. So if you have a passion, carry out a little research on the web to see if there is a charity or organization that you could support.

Your Home

" Why should I care about future generations? What have they ever done for me? "

Groucho Marx

Chapter 6
Your Home

Our house is our home and, for many of us, our home reflects the people we are. It's somewhere we use to retreat from the madness of the outside world. Hopefully it is also one of the few places we have total control of what goes on. So it is one of the few places on this planet we can really help make a difference by changing little things that will collectively make a big difference.

Make do and mend

Next time your vacuum cleaner, washing machine, etc. breaks down don't smile because you now have the perfect excuse to buy that super deluxe, all singing, all dancing machine next door has. See if you can get it mended and, if you can't, do you really need a new one? How about saving your cash and help the environment by purchasing a re-conditioned one?

Old wives' tales

Have you ever looked at the ingredients of all those cleaning products jostling for space in your cupboard? You'll be horrified at some of them, especially once you read the safety precautions. So try a few of those old cleaning tips, vinegar for windows and mirrors for example? You'll save yourself a little money and cause less damage to the environment.

Flick that switch

Our homes are filled with power guzzling devices, washing machines, televisions, computers, DVD players; the list goes on and on. Now, even whilst sitting there doing nothing, when turned on they're using electricity, so by flicking that switch to off you cut down on the amount of electricity being used, which is good for both pocket and planet.

Turn it on its head

You've come to the dregs at the bottom of the bottle but you can still see a little shampoo, face cream, liquid hand wash, etc. clinging to the base. You know there is at least another one or two dollops left, so to get at them simply turn the bottle on its head and allow them to slowly work themselves down. Then, once it's truly empty, you can pop it into the recycle bin.

GREEN FACT

Just one recycled can saves enough energy to run a television for three hours.

Let's go thermal

If you invest and install a thermal solar heater, did you know that you would get around 70% of your hot water totally free? Not bad!

6 inches is how big?

To ensure your newly fitted loft insulation works it needs to be at least 6″ (15cm) thick.

A little light on the matter

Once upon a time, energy saving light bulbs had bad press as they gave off poor light and weren't very environmentally sound in their production.

As 'green' technology has improved so have energy saving bulbs. And the beauty of these is they not only last longer (meaning you have to change them less often), they also use less energy, so save you some cash. They come in a huge variety of styles and mounts so you're sure to find one that suits your needs.

No weakling

If your batteries are getting to the end of their life, they may still be strong enough to operate something that requires less energy, your TV remote for example. Get the very last little bit of 'juice' out of them before you send them to the cycling center or go one better and get yourself some rechargeable batteries and a solar powered battery charger.

GREEN FACT

In July 2007, the Vatican City became the first carbon neutral state in the world; the goal was reached through the donation of the Vatican Climate Forest in Hungary. The forest is large enough to offset a year's carbon dioxide emissions.

Do you have to go up a size?

Is your home feeling a little on the small side? You may find a simple de-clutter will help. Give away, donate, and recycle all those things you don't need. Books that sit on the shelf unread, DVD's not watched, games not played. Or why not make yourself some money and have a garage sale.

Line up

Lining your curtains with thermal linings will not only increase the life of your curtains but will cut down on the light they allow through. It will also cut your energy bills by reducing the amount of heat that escapes through those windows on cold days and nights. Also, during the cold winter months, close your curtains as soon as it begins to get dark and you'll cut down on heat loss.

Layer up

When it's cold, rather than whacking up the thermostat on your heater, try digging out that jumper and putting that on instead. Or if you find it's getting too hot in the summer then leave the windows closed and shut the curtains. Believe it or not it will actually stop the heat from coming in and the house will feel much cooler.

All change

Even if you haven't changed to energy saving light bulbs, there are other ways you can cut down on your energy consumption. Use a lower wattage light bulb or change to fluorescent, which uses less energy than a conventional light bulb. Also think about the lights you turn on. In our kitchen, like many, we have a main light plus lights under the cupboards. Although these look pretty they really are pointless, so they don't get turned on most of the time.

Home maintenance

With a little home maintenance just where it counts you can not only cut your costs but also be a little greener. For example, stop that dripping tap and save up to 20 gallons (90 liters) of water a year.

Cold case

Every time you open the door to your fridge or freezer you are losing precious cold. So don't take out the milk, remove the lid, pour it on your breakfast cereal, put the milk back in the fridge and then close the door! Take the milk out and close the door. You may think it's only a few seconds but add those up over a year and you'll be surprised at how much that habit is costing you.

"Suburbia is where the developer bulldozes out the trees, then names the streets after them. "

Bill Vaughn

Keep an eye

It's only when you come to pay your bill that you realize just how much electricity you've used. However, there are devices that can keep track of what you use. You can then try to reduce your consumption. So whatever you spend on the gadget, you'll soon claw it back by the energy you save.

What are you sitting on?

Buying new furniture is a chore at the best of times, with the whole household having to agree what is comfortable and what is not, what looks cool and what does not, etc.

Trying to think green when making such a large purchase can be a nightmare. However, more and more designers and manufacturers are making furniture from materials that are renewable and even recycled. So next time you're thinking about replacing your furniture why not think green?

One of the three Rs

Buying new furniture has already been mentioned but do you really have to go new? Try looking for something 'new' at the local charity or thrift shop, or go upmarket and buy antique (which simply means second hand but really old). However, do take care when buying these types of items and ensure they are free from life forms like woodworm.

No to shoes

By simply taking off your shoes as soon as you walk into the house, you'll keep your carpets looking nicer longer, requiring less vacuuming and cleaning. You'll also cut down on the amount of 'nasty things' you can bring into the house.

> **❝** The struggle to save the global environment is in one way much more difficult than the struggle to vanquish Hitler, for this time the war is with ourselves. We are the enemy, just as we have only ourselves as allies. **❞**

Al Gore, Former US Vice-President

Sweet smell

We all like to make our homes smell good. However, instead of using chemical-based sprays or plug-in air fresheners, try some of these alternatives:

- Place a small bowl of vinegar hidden out of the way and it will deodorize a room where people have smoked.

- Burning candles can also remove the smell of cigarette smoke.

- Place slices of lemon in a pan and bring to the boil for a zesty fresh smell, or try cinnamon instead.

- Essential oils burned in an oil burner will add a nice smell to the room. They can also help sleep (lavender), clear the nose (eucalyptus), or help the thinking process (rosemary).

- Make an old fashioned pomander using fruit and cloves.

- Baking soda dissolved in water will absorb bad smells.

- To freshen drains, pour down some baking soda then add a cup of white vinegar. The two will begin to bubble, and when this stops flush both away with some hot water.

- Reduce the smell coming from the nappy/diaper bin by first dumping any of the natural waste in the toilet and flush.

- A waterproof container containing some used, wet coffee grounds is great for removing stale odors in small rooms and the car as the grounds absorb any nasty whiffs. If you are using in a car, remember to remove them before you start any journey.

Foiled again

If you want to increase the efficiency of your radiators then place foil (shiny side out) behind them to bounce the heat back into the room. Also, if you have a radiator under a window, much of the heat can be lost, so put a shelf over the radiator and the heat will be funneled into the room rather than disappearing out of the window.

GREEN FACT

It has been estimated that 8% of electricity used by appliances in the average home is used whilst they are sitting in standby mode, and the average home has 12 devices that can sit flickering away in the corner of a room. This puts an extra 1 million metric tons of CO_2 into the atmosphere each year.

Go a little bit crazy

If you're looking for fun ways to make shelving and don't want to purchase wood, then check out this video: **www.videojug.com/film/how-to-install-invisible-shelves**. It not only cuts down on the cost but it's a great way of recycling an old book. They also have other ideas including using old CD covers for shelving. So spend some time watching and get inspired.

The beauty of baking soda

You'd not believe what baking soda can do! It's not only good for adding to your cooking but a great alternative to those horrible cleaning products. Here are just some of the uses:

- Get the gleam back on your taps and chrome by mixing a little water with baking soda to form a paste.

- Clean your fridge with a solution of three tablespoons of baking soda dissolved in half a cup of warm water and then wipe over with a damp cloth.

- Place half a cup of baking soda, followed by half a cup of vinegar, washed down with boiling water, the mixture will unblock that drain.

- Remove coffee and tea stains from cups by soaking in a little baking soda.

- Place baking soda in a bowl and it'll soak up those nasty niffs in the refrigerator.

- If you need to clean your microwave, place two tablespoons of baking soda in water in a large microwavable container. Allow to boil for a few moments then wipe the inside surfaces with a damp cloth.

- Make a paste using warm water and baking soda and use it to clean the inside of your dishwasher. After application wipe down with a damp cloth.

- Place five teaspoons of baking soda mixed with hot water in the bowl of your toilet. Allow it to sit overnight and along with removing any nasty stains you also have a clean smelling toilet.

- When you empty the bin, sprinkle a little baking soda in the bottom to keep it smelling fresh.

- Add two heaped tablespoons of baking soda to your normal dish washer powder and it'll cut down on the grease and food left on dishes, pans and inside the washer itself.

- I have checked with a fire officer and apparently baking soda, if scattered on a small fire, will help extinguish it. This method will not work on liquid fires.

- Place half a cup of soda into your washing machine each and every wash and it will help remove the build up of oil and grease in your clothes.

- When you change your cat or dog's litter tray cover the bottom of the box with baking soda. This will help adsorb some of the odor given off.

- Next time you have to wash out your thermos flask or cool drink bottles rinse with a little soda and warm water.

- When you've cut onions or crushed garlic, simply wet your hands and rub some baking soda over them then rinse in warm water to remove the smell.

Kitchen and Bathroom

" We never know the worth of water till the well is dry. "

Author Unknown

Chapter 7
Kitchen and Bathroom

If there are two rooms in the house where being green is the hardest it is perhaps the kitchen and the bathroom. However, with the following tips, you'll be able to make a start at being green and save yourself some cash in the bargain!

For ladies only

Whatever term you use for it, most women have to deal with their period. Although convenient, tampons and towels create a large amount of waste. There is an alternative to the throw away tampon which is a reusable, washable menstrual cup. When using this, you remove the risk of toxic shock syndrome associated with tampons and save yourself money. Now if you can't bring yourself to use one then just changing to organic cotton tampons will make a difference – remember to put them in the bin rather than down the toilet, it'll stop you seeing them again on the beach!

Toothbrushes

We're told we should change our toothbrushes every six months, which for our oral hygiene is great but for the typical toothbrush is just so wasteful. It's the head that gets worn out not the handle. So it makes little sense to throw something away that isn't worn out. So guess what? You can actually buy brushes where you can reuse the handle again and again by simply attaching a new head. The simple ideas always seem to be the best.

All blocked up

Next time your sink gets blocked, rather than reach for a bottle of chemicals, try a good old baking soda and vinegar solution. If the sink is full of water, bail it out, pour one cup of baking soda down the plug hole, and then one cup of vinegar on top of this; quickly put the plug in place. After half an hour or so pour a kettleful of hot water down the drain. One unclogged sink without harsh chemicals. It really works!

Cold spell

Electrical appliances that create heat or reduce heat (cool things) are the worst offenders for wasting electricity. However, to help your refrigerator and freezer operate better simply defrost them on a regular basis. Also the way in which they are packed can help them be more efficient; basically, ensure they are packed tightly. If your appliance is a little on the old side then invest in a device that can sense when your refrigerator or freezer does not need energy. The device cleverly adjusts what is being taken, lowering energy consumption.

Beach wear

Next time you flush a little something down your toilet, give a thought to our beaches. In 2010, 14 CUB Scouts spent just 20 minutes picking litter up on a local beach (Kilcreggan beach – Scotland) and found an incredible 2,500 cotton bud sticks. If you would like to discover more about what amazing items are floating in our seas visit: **http://5gyres.org/**

These are obviously not only unsightly and cost money to pick up, but they are also detrimental to the environment.

" When drinking water,
remember its source. **"**

Chinese Proverb

Cooking up a steam

How often have you placed a small pan on the biggest ring on your cooker? Did you know that by this simple action you are wasting around 40% of the heat given off? So match the size of the pan to the size of the ring. You can also cut down on cooking times if you change your cooking habits. For example, if you're planning rice and vegetables, part cook the rice then add the vegetables and let the lot cook in the same pan. Or rather than hard boiling an egg, which can take eight to ten minutes, try poaching, which normally only takes three minutes.

Toilet talk

The average family flushes two bath tubs of water down the toilet each day. To cut down on this water, take the advice given in the film Meet The Fockers by the character, Bernie Focker played by Dustin Hoffman, "If it's yellow let it mellow, if it's brown flush it down."

Turn it down

By turning the temperature down on your washing machine to 30°C you can reduce the energy consumption by a massive 40%. This means you'll save enough energy in a year to watch 1,400 episodes of your favorite TV soap or boil enough water to make 2,500 cups of your favorite hot drinks! If you refrain from these activities as well, you'll save the same amount of CO_2 as you would have spent when driving 150 miles (241.5km) in the average family car.

Tea total

When you make yourself a cup of tea or coffee, just use the water you need. Or why not try replacing one hot drink with a cold drink each day? It doesn't sound a lot but over a year that's a lot of kettles that have gone un-boiled!

Concentrate now!

Buying your cleaning products as concentrates means you use less packaging, throw less away and the manufacturers have to ship less, cutting down on emissions created by transportation. However, you can go further and switch to products that are environmentally friendly. One product (EcoBalls®) allows you to wash your clothes with the aid of ionized oxygen. This process activates the water molecules naturally and allows them to penetrate deep into clothing fibers to lift dirt away, which means you don't have to use fabric conditioner. P.S. for the sceptical: after much deliberation I took the plunge and my clothes have never looked back.

Sweet smell

When using alternatives to washing powder, your clothes will no longer have that 'clean fresh' smell the adverts go on about. So should you wish to 'freshen' up your laundry then you could add a couple of drops of lavender oil to the rinse cycle. Also, if there are stubborn stains then good old baking powder added to the wash cycle will give the cleaning process a boost.

Make it a game

On average, taking a bath uses 17½ gallons (80 liters) of water whereas a shower will take about half that amount. To encourage the kids to shower, make a game of it. Who can get the cleanest in just three minutes? This will not only save you water but think of the time it'll save at 'bath' time. Another way to save water is to use a cup of water for cleaning your teeth rather than a running tap. It sounds so easy but how many of us do it?

Shower power

Although showers are a great way of saving water, they can get grubby very quickly. So rather than reaching for chemicals, try these alternatives:

- Shower curtains can be cleaned with distilled vinegar then rinsed with warm water.

- If you want to stop the bottom of the curtain from becoming moldy, try coating it with baby oil.

- Don't throw away that leftover half glass of white wine; use it to clean the glass on the shower door.

- Reuse those sheets of fabric conditioner and rub them over shower doors to get rid of soap scum.

- Soak the shower head overnight in vinegar and the scale will be removed.

Oven ready

Rather than having to clean your oven each and every time you use it, simply line it with aluminium foil. This will catch all the grease, etc. and cut down on the need for using cleaners. This neat little trick can also be used for the grill pan.

Love the label

Next time you're buying any product, check the label. If the company respects the environment they'll shout it via their label. There are a number of reliable green labeling schemes covering everything from food, clothes, and household appliances. It's now getting easier to make a green choice.

Grate news

To help with the cleaning of graters, rub the surface with a little vegetable oil before use. Then, once used, rub a hard crust of bread over it to help clean it. If it is really mucky then an old tooth brush will easily get into those little nooks and crannies.

Fantastic floors!

Next time you get the urge to wash your floor, rather than using a bucket, use your bin. That way when you rinse it out you'll be doing two jobs at once! The bin will also smell fresh and clean without the need to use extra cleaning products.

Clean, clean, clean

To get the best results from your fridge or freezer, ensure the coils at the back are kept clean. Simply unplug, pull forward a little then use the fine hose on your vacuum cleaner to suck up all that dust and dirt. It'll not only help your appliance perform better but should also increase its life.

Sorry stainless sink

If your sink needs a bit of a clean then there are several quick and easy ways to do it without chemicals:

- Baking soda made into a paste will easily remove any stubborn mark.

- For a quick clean simply sprinkle with baking soda, wipe with a sponge, then remove with warm water.

- Once your sink is clean, rub over with a page of scrunched up newspaper to get rid of water marks.

- If you have hard water then neat white vinegar left on for half an hour will lift that lime scale.

" The packaging for a microwavable 'microwave' dinner is programmed for a shelf life of maybe six months, a cook time of two minutes and a landfill dead-time of centuries. "

David Wann, Buzzworm

Potty over potatoes

To extend the life of your potatoes, keep them in a brown paper bag in a cool dark place. If they do start to look a little sorry for themselves then cook, mash and put in the freezer. This then makes a quick alternative when you're pushed for time.

Exciting eggs

If the sell-by date on your eggs has come and gone, there is a way to check to see if they are still okay to eat. Fill a jug with water then place the egg in the water. If the egg sits on the bottom it's fine. If it stands on its end, although not fresh, it should still be okay to eat. However, if the egg floats then it has gone off.

Terrific tomatoes

If you find your tomatoes have gone a little soft then freeze them rather than consign them to the compost heap. Freeze individually and although you'll not be able to use them for a fresh salad they can be added to any cooked dish requiring tomatoes.

Food for thought

There are apparently three main reasons why we throw away food. These are:

- Cooking and preparing too much.

- Allowing fruit and vegetables to become over-ripe.

- Allowing them to go off, and not eating food before the use-by date.

To overcome these:

- Plan what you're going to eat and keep an eye on those sell-by dates.

- If foodstuff looks like it is going off and it can be frozen, put it in the freezer until it's needed.

- If you've cooked too much, don't put it on the plate. Either put it into the fridge for use later or into the freezer.

- Store food appropriately; for example, things stay much fresher if kept in an air-tight container.

- Find ways to use the food you have. For example, stale bread can be turned into bread pudding or over-ripe fruit can be used in a pie. A great website for ideas on how to use and store left over food is **www.lovefoodhatewaste.com**

Lovely bubbly

Those little dregs of wine and beer needn't be thrown away. Pour them into ice cube makers, freeze and then add to casseroles, stews and the like to give your food a little kick.

Bath time

A shower reduces the amount of water we use but a long soak in a bath is nice! So to cut down on some of that guilt:

- Bathe with someone else!

- Don't pull the plug but use a bucket so you can reuse the water in your garden.

- Go the whole hog and look into 'grey water recycling,' this is where the water from your bath, shower and laundry are used to flush your toilet.

As nature intended

For a great complexion: drink your four pints (two and a half liters) of water a day and your complexion will thank you for it. A good complexion means less foundation!

> **"** There are 70 pesticides that are listed as known or probable carcinogens, based on animal testing. Of those 70, 44 are in use today, and 23 are used on our food. **"**

Gina Solomon, Specialist in Internal Medicine

Sweet smell

The average bottle of perfume could contain up to 600 synthetic chemicals (how do they get so many in one little bottle?). So try natural perfumes or aromatherapy oils instead. But be aware, to call themselves natural they only need a small amount of natural ingredient in them, so read the label with care.

Tried and tested

Steer clear of products that have been tested on animals. Look at the label and be aware that just because it says 'not tested on animals' it doesn't mean that the ingredients have not been. Look out for the relevant symbol or the wording 'our products and their ingredients are not animal tested.' One symbol to look for is the Humane Cosmetics Standard 'rabbit and stars' symbol. This is recognized worldwide and tells you the product and its ingredients have not been tested on animals. To find out more check out: http://www.eceae.org/index.php

Average Joe's carbon footprint

- Private transport (let's be honest – our cars) is 10%

- What we eat and drink is 5%

- Our homes (the building itself and the furniture, etc.) is 9%

- Our leisure time is 14%

- Our share of using public services is 12%

- Our personal gadgets and what we wear make up 4%

- Our use of fossil fuel and electricity is a staggering 27%

- Miscellaneous (flights, the making of our car, our finances, etc.) is 16%

- And just 3% is public transport

- Christmas food: 26kg of CO_2 per person

- Travel by car at Christmas: 96kg of CO_2 per person

- Extravagant Christmas lighting: 218kg of CO_2 per person

- Christmas shopping: 310kg of CO_2 per person

- A vegetarian Christmas would result in a saving of 3kg of CO_2 per person

- Go organic; just 50% of food being organic would save 2kg of CO_2 per person

- You could save 7kg of CO_2 per person if you aimed to have a low waste Christmas

In the Workplace

❝ Modern technology owes ecology an apology. **❞**

Alan M. Eddison

Chapter 8
In the Workplace

You've become really good at home but when it comes to your work place it all goes to 'pot' and all those good intentions go out the window. We all do it, expecting someone else to set the ball rolling. So take hold of your convictions and take hold of that ball and roll it along the length of the office, you'll be surprised at how soon other people will join you.

Water, water everywhere...

Don't use bottled water in the office, invest in a filter jug. Per liter bottled water is perhaps one of the most expensive fluids you can buy; some boffin has worked out that several brands are even more expensive than a good bottle of bubbly.

Do you need another coffee?

The standard kettle takes about 2000 watts of electrical power and, on average, takes three minutes to boil if full. That's a lot of energy and a waste of time compared with pouring yourself a much healthier drink of water or fruit juice. Obviously the water is straight from the tap or if you're a little fussy then filtered in a jug and not out of a plastic bottle.

Laptop versus desktop

A laptop computer uses 15 watts to 45 watts of electricity per hour on average compared to the average desktop computer (with a 17″ CRT monitor) which uses anything between 60 watts to 250 watts. So in energy consumption the laptop beats the desktop hands down!

Paper trial

Another way to reduce the amount of paper we use (and obviously the cost of buying paper) is to send more documents via e-mail and save these files on the computer. This will also save you space, as you'll be cutting down on the need for filing cabinets. Remember to ensure your files are backed up on a regular basis and copies of files are kept off site.

Lights out!

How often have you walked passed an office block with each floor lit up like a Christmas tree? Get the boss to invest in motion sensors, dimmers and timers. These will turn the lights off when not in use and if someone wanders around, the motion sensors will light the room and let the world know they're there. Any installation costs will soon be recouped with the saving on the lower light bill.

Not so fantastic plastic

How many of us take our drinks at work in paper, plastic, or polystyrene cups but would not dream of doing so at home? Bring in a mug from home, which, with the aid of a little water and washing up liquid (environmentally sound of course), can be used again and again.

E-mail extras

When printing an e-mail, rather than printing the whole 'conversation' just print off the bits that you need. Simply highlight the section of interest, then print choosing 'selection.'

Natural light

Rather than having to put the lights on all the time because you have files running the length of the window sill, simply remove those files, pull up those blinds and make use of all that natural free light.

66 It is good to realize that if love and peace can prevail on earth, and if we can teach our children to honor nature's gifts, the joys and beauties of the outdoors will be here forever. **99**

Jimmy Carter

An extra R: Rewritable

Rather than buying and using CDs once, invest in rewritables. These can be used time and time again. Simply wipe clean when not needed, relabel and use again. You'll be saving on wasted CDs, saving yourself cash and the headache of what to do with a CD that holds sensitive information.

It's a copy

When making copies from books or magazines, rather than copying full size, scale down and copy two pages onto one A4 sheet. If you're worried you'll not be able to read the text at half the size then copy full size but use both sides of the paper.

When not in use

Many rooms in a building are not used for long periods of time, for example, meeting rooms, kitchen areas, and toilets. So why leave the lights on? A quick flick of the switch is all it needs.

Now wash your hands

Most, if not all, toilets have a little sign telling you to wash your hands. Very sensible advice but drying them on paper towels is a waste of resources. Invest in a hand drier. There are lots on the market and the new options are getting better and better at drying hands and using less energy.

Come prepared

Rather than popping out of the office to buy your sandwich, why not make your own? It'll cut down on the costs of your meal and the waste of packaging used.

Recycle here

Set up a recycling system in your office, including everything from those nasty plastic bottles to cans, cartridges and paper. Then contact the local authority and set up a collection of all that lovely recyclable stuff.

Shout it from the roof tops

Today people like to see companies taking action when it comes to green issues. So get the boss on board and once your office or company starts to implement green procedures, make sure it goes into the newsletter, as a fact in the footer of letters, and on the company website. In today's competitive environment if you can show you're doing something good for the environment you may just win that important client, who based their decision on your green credentials.

Shop around

Shop around for companies that supply your energy needs, your communicating needs, and office supply needs. If they're not as green as you then change to a company that is.

If you have to

If you have to use polystyrene cups, don't throw them away. Believe it or not they can be recycled and turned into stationery that you can then buy back and use around the office.

❝ I wake up in the morning asking myself what can I do today, how can I help the world today. I believe in what I do beyond a shadow of a doubt. I gave my word to this tree and to all the people that my feet would not touch the ground until I had done everything in my power to make the world aware of this problem and to stop the destruction. **❞**

Julia Butterfly Hill (environmentalist who spent 738 days living in a tree in order to save the old growth forests)

Fair trade

The amount of tea, coffee, and hot chocolate drunk in the office each week is staggering. So get the person in charge of buying supplies to look into changing to drinks that are labeled fair trade. By switching you can make a real difference to the lives of those who struggle on almost slave wages. These farmers can then help conserve their environment in turn, safe in the knowledge that they are earning enough to support themselves and their families.

Caring is sharing

Most people in the office will start and finish at the same time. Some may even live within walking distance of one another. So rather than each driving a car to work, set up a car share system, perhaps taking it in turns to drive into work; this'll cut down CO_2 emissions and cut down on everyone's fuel bill.

Business travel

Today, communication across many miles is easier than ever. So does all that business travel really need to take place? Think long and hard before that plane is booked or you jump into that car. Video conferencing is surely the way forward. It also makes sense as less of the working day is spent in traffic jams or checking in luggage, making sure your time spent is much more productive.

Source at home

When looking to make a purchase, spend a little time to see if you can acquire it from a local source. You'll not only be supporting your local economy but also cutting down on the costs and wasted energy in transporting the goods.

Try mending

Next time something breaks down, rather than think 'we'll buy new' see if you can get it mended, or check in the cupboard to see if you already have something stashed away you forgot about. If you are not able to get it mended, check to see if there is somewhere it can go where the components can be recycled. Or if it is an item that will only be needed for a few months, consider hiring rather than buying.

Work from home

Check to see if your boss will allow you to work from home. It's easy to set up communications between home and office and for some people they find it easier to get on with things rather than deal with the distractions of the office. For your boss, it will mean higher productivity, for you it'll be a saving on travel time, and the planet will thank you for the reduced CO_2 emissions.

Make yourself a good name

The best form of advertising is word of mouth, so don't throw out old equipment; see if a local school, charity or voluntary organization could benefit from a donation. Donate your used printer cartridges to help raise funds, keep postage stamps and again donate. Wood from old furniture could be used by the art students at a local college; also items like CDs, packaging (including bubble wrap), etc. could be used as art material. You'll soon get yourself known as a company that cares, and people like to deal with companies that care.

GREEN FACTS

Some scary facts taken from www.christianaid.org.uk

- The 1990s were the hottest recorded since records began and this temperature rise is speeding up. The world's surface temperatures are rising more rapidly than at any point in the last 10,000 years.

- Over the past 35 years, hurricanes like Hurricane Katrina have almost doubled in number. Meteorologists warn that rises in the temperature of the sea surface are the most likely cause.

- Since 1850, a period in which today's richest countries have industrialized rapidly, levels of CO_2 have risen 28% and methane levels are 112% higher.

Power of the sun

When you need to invest in new equipment, see if you can harness the power of the sun. For example, solar powered calculators will cut down on the use of batteries. If small appliances are used 'out in the field' invest in those with solar power chargers.

Get it serviced

Having machines serviced on a regular basis will ensure they run at optimum efficiency. This also goes for lighting! Did you know that flickering fluorescent tubes take more energy than ones in good working order? Once changed, don't throw them away as the mercury in them can be reclaimed.

The power of the pen

When buying office products, think about purchasing refillable pens rather than use-once biros. If you have to purchase biros, choose ones that are made from materials that will biodegrade (such as corn starch). You could even source pencils that are made from mouse mats or car tires.

" A person with a new idea is a crank until the idea succeeds. "

Mark Twain

Cut down

Does your company actually create a product that is shipped? Then take a look at your packaging. It may cost a little to adjust the packaging, but by cutting down you'll lessen the amount that goes to landfill, showing your commitment to all that is green and also cutting the costs and increasing the profits.

GREEN FACTS

Did you know that 15% of your air conditioning costs and those horrid greenhouse gas emissions are directly related to the heat produced by your office equipment and lighting. So turn off whenever possible!

If your office has a foyer and that foyer has just 15 halogen lights you can reduce your annual CO_2 emissions by 485lbs (220kg) by turning them off just one hour earlier each night.

A shocking 50% of your office waste is made up of all that paperwork!

For every 2lbs (1kg) of food disposed of in landfill, just under the same amount of CO_2 is produced. So when catering try to avoid food that, if it goes uneaten, cannot be easily stored.

For more facts, figures and ideas visit:
http://www.abc.net.au/greenatwork/FactsFigures/

DIY

66 If a man walks in the woods for love of them half of each day, he is in danger of being regarded as a loafer. But if he spends his days as a speculator, shearing off those woods and making the earth bald before her time, he is deemed an industrious and enterprising citizen. 99

Henry David Thoreau: Author and Naturalist (1817–1862)

Chapter 9
DIY

Some of us love it and some of us hate it, but however hard we try, even the smallest of DIY jobs cannot be escaped. So next time you get out that hammer, nail or paint brush give yourself a pat on the back when you know you're also taking the environment into consideration.

Can't see the wood for the trees

Try to choose wood products made from sustainable wood. This is far easier now than it used to be. You simply have to look for the labels, the Forest Stewardship Council (FSC) certifies over 39 million hectares of forest in 66 different countries for example. Another label to look out for is the Programme for the Endorsement of Forest Certification schemes (PEFC).

The borrowers

The borrowers are not just little people who live under your floorboards and come out each night to borrow what they need. Even you can be a borrower and your excuse (sorry, reason) is because it is greener. Did you know that on average the drill living under your stairs or hidden in your shed will only be used for 15 minutes in its whole life? That's just mad! So find out what your family and friends have stashed away, make a list and then share that list. Then everyone will know who to ask when they next have that little odd job.

Through the roof!

Around half the heat lost in your home escapes through the walls and roof. So invest in cavity wall insulation and loft insulation. It is also important to remember to use the right stuff! Again, with a little shopping around you'll find all manner of insulation made from recycled materials, including old newspapers and even jeans.

Light is right

When you get the chance to change the color of your walls, go for light colors. These not only lift the spirits, make the room look cleaner but also bounce more light around the room. In this way you'll find you have to turn on the lights less. Also, if you go for window treatments that can be pulled back during the day, you'll have loads of light flooding in.

Go designer

Rather than looking for items that have been shipped hundreds, if not thousands, of miles, see if you can find a local supplier who could make that fitted cupboard for you. Many smaller businesses also offer a service where they can turn your design into reality. You may be surprised; you might also save yourself some cash. A number of years ago I approached a local blacksmith after I'd seen a couple of his candlesticks. Well, he called them candlesticks, but they were really works of art. After a quick chat, he was more than willing to make my dining table and chairs, sourcing everything locally. I got the exact table to fit my needs, within the budget I had set and it only traveled 15 miles.

Drafts are daft

Draft proofing your home is a great way to cut down on your energy costs. Why pay for heating that can simply escape through ill-fitting windows and doors? You can also make some of the draft proofing yourself. For example, the old fashioned stuffed toy dachshund made from an old shirt against each door will help.

66 I think the environment should be put in the category of our national security. Defence of our resources is just as important as defence abroad. Otherwise what is there to defend? **99**

Robert Redford, Yosemite National Park dedication

Forward thinking

Next time you purchase flat-pack furniture and start to put it together, rather than use glue or nails, use screws instead. This will allow you to take the item apart with ease and take it with you should you move.

Reuse

When you rip something out or take something apart try to think out of the box and see if you can come up with an ingenious way of reusing it. Some years ago I was looking for a worktop for the shed. My neighbor pulled out the side of an old wardrobe and suggested I use that. It does the job and cost me nothing!!!

Put on a jacket

As previously mentioned, putting on an extra layer will cut down on the fuel costs and this also goes for your boiler. Insulating your boiler with a jacket will keep your water hotter for longer. Also, if your boiler is over fifteen years old, it may be time to change it for one that is more energy efficient.

Titillating tiles

If you have a tiling job, rather than popping along and purchasing tiles made from virgin resources, go for recycled glass and porcelain. They look just as good and can be the talking point of that new kitchen.

Remember your BUDDies

B: Buy only what you need

U: Use everything you buy

D: Donate left-over's

D: Dispose of waste responsibly

Second hand rose

Items don't have to be brand new. Why not visit the local charity shops or see if you can bag a bargain at the local auctions.

Plant power

When adding the finishing touches to your new room, think plants. They are great natural air filters and if you have used paints that give off VOCs they'll help remove them.

Clean as you go

We've all done it, left a paint brush sitting on the side until its gone rock hard so it can't be used. Try to get into the habit of cleaning as you go and that brush will last and last. Also resist reaching for those paint cleaners. Many carry a skull and crossbones; I'd take that as a small warning that they're bad! So a few tips for those brushes:

- Reduce the amount of paint that dries on the head of the paint brush by dampening first in water, if you are using oil-based paint dip it into paint thinner.

- If you take a break, wrap the brush in a damp cloth or put it into a plastic bag to stop the paint from drying.

- To clean, fill an old paint tin with warm soapy water, put the brush into the water and move backwards and forwards vigorously, put it in clean water and repeat. This should remove all of the paint.

- If a brush does stiffen up, try soaking in hot vinegar and then combing through with an old fork.

" A society is defined not only by what it creates, but by what it refuses to destroy. "

John Sawhill, Former President/CEO of The Nature Conservancy

X marks the spot

Don't decide you're going to redecorate a whole room just because of a few marks on the wall. Instead you could:

- Try moving the furniture so they are hidden or, if it is just one mark, find a wall hanging, poster or picture that can be hung over the offending mark.

- Fit some shelving over the mark.

- On emulsion, most stains can be removed by using a mild washing detergent (the type you use for delicate clothes) mixed 50:50 with warm water.

GREEN FACT
By installing or fitting some form of insulation, each home could cut their carbon emission by half.

Fabulous floors

The range of flooring available is a minefield. What to pick? Carpets are often backed with PVC, which is very slow to decompose in landfill. They are also known to trap dust and other little nasties that can aggravate conditions like asthma. So try going for something natural, like sea grass or jute. If you decide to go for wood flooring then check that it has the relevant labels or go along to your local salvage yard and see if they have something you can use. To find out more about different floor treatments that offer benefits to allergy sufferers visit **www.healthyflooring.org**

Become PC with your WC

If you're about to invest in a new bathroom or shower, then fit a low-flush toilet to cut down on water usage. By fitting low-flow aerators to taps or fitting low-flow shower heads, you can again save water. This not only cuts down on your water usage but, if you're not using as much hot water, you do not have to heat as much. So you're saving on your heating bills as well. Also, did you know that you can get waterless urinals?

Plastered!

I'm not talking about one too many drinks but the plaster you use on walls. Now did you know you can get plaster that is already colored? Think about it, a newly plastered wall you don't have to paint!

Don't let's skirt around it

If you have to replace the skirting boards then invest in a skirting board that doubles up as a heater. They not only save you space (because you can get rid of that ugly radiator) but also cash, because they are more energy efficient.

Great with glass

When you're changing interior walls, don't just think brick or plasterboard, think glass bricks. They have great sound and heat insulation qualities and also allow you to take advantage of all that lovely free light that streams through. Insure that the wall is not load bearing and that the floor can take the extra weight.

GREEN FACT

It is believed that 70% of plants found in the world's forests could have medicinal properties. At the rate we are losing forests, we'll never discover many of them.

Light fantastic

As you are redecorating, take the opportunity to change the way you light your home. Use energy efficient lighting where possible and make the most of the lighting you're installing, try to avoid decorative lighting, which may look pretty but will cost you money each and every time you flick that switch.

If it's good enough for Pandas

Bamboo is the ultimate in cheap and eco-friendly building materials. It grows three times faster than other materials, such as wood. As it grows it releases 30% more oxygen than trees, and very few pesticides are used in order to grow it. An all round winner!

PVC ban

When replacing windows or pipes, try to avoid using PVC. Unfortunately, the process of making PVC is highly toxic and it also produces by-products that are hazardous to health and the environment.

Top of the class

When having your dream kitchen or bathroom fitted, granite or marble looks great. However, the quarrying for these luxury items cause immense environmental damage, so look for alternatives, such as recycled glass or reclaimed wood.

Wall to wall

Rather than using wall-to-wall carpet, give carpet tiles a go. If you have an accident you can replace just one tile rather than changing the whole thing. Also, there are many companies that now offer tiles made from recycled materials.

Do you have to start from scratch?

Years ago I wanted a new kitchen. I'd always wanted a blue and yellow kitchen; don't ask me why, I just did. Unfortunately, we didn't have the money to start from scratch so I found a local company who would supply just the doors. I got my new look kitchen with blue cupboard doors for a third of the price and I saved on the cost and time of having a new kitchen fitted.

Useful Websites

The following sites range from those that allow you to swap and donate unwanted goods to companies that sell environmentally friendly products. This is obviously not a definitive list but will hopefully help you on your way to making those small changes.

Please note we cannot vouch for any of the services offered and benefits claimed by any site on this list.

www.honestycosmetics.co.uk

Products are endorsed by The Vegan Society, BUAV Humane Cosmetics Standard, the Ethical Company Organization Good Shopping Guide and the Naturewatch Trust Compassionate Shopping Guide.

www.glowing-skin-naturally.com

Sells Natural Skin Care, natural body care products and related natural lifestyle products.

www.savawatt.co.uk

Sells a product called SavaPlug, which can help you cut down on the energy consumption of refrigerators and freezers.

www.littlesatsuma.com

Small 'green' manufacturer of soap and other related items that avoid the use of palm oil and harsh chemicals.

www.earthbornpaints.co.uk

Produces a range of natural paints, varnishes and flooring products, some of which use organic ingredients and are VOC (Volatile Organic Compounds) free.

www.livingsoil.co.uk

Living Soil provides all natural, probiotic-based products for home and garden, human health, agriculture, waste and septic treatment, and environmental sustainability.

www.communityrepaint.org.uk

Helps you donate paint by providing a searchable database for projects in need of your leftover and unwanted paint.

www.wigglywigglers.co.uk

A company that encourages you to garden with wildlife in mind by selling a wide range of gardening products.

www.mini-organic.co.uk

Sells a range of organic baby clothes and organic clothing for children, ethically manufactured from organic cotton in the UK and India, all clothes are certified organic either by Agreco or SKAL.

www.auro.co.uk

Produces a range of natural paints and varnishes.

www.energysavingtrust.org.uk

Provides information on how to save energy.

www.goreal.org.uk

Provides a solution to the throwaway nappy/diaper.

www.natll.org.uk

The site for the National Association of Toy & Leisure Libraries.

www.ecokettle.com

A kettle that allows you to just boil the water you need, no more and no less.

www.mooncup.co.uk

Provides a solution to the throw away tampon.

www.uk.freecycle.org

Freecycle groups match people who have things they want to get rid of with people who can use them.

www.u-exchange.com

Swap items you don't want for items that you do.

www.greenlivingtips.com

Full of articles all about ways to live a greener lifestyle.

www.rspb.org.uk/hfw

Ideas and tips on making homes for wildlife in your garden.

www.pioneerthinking.com

Full of great ideas and recipes for making your own products from insect repellents to shampoos.

www.recycledproducts.org.uk

Helps you find all manner of products made from recycled and reused materials.

www.direct.gov.uk/en/ Environmentandgreenerliving

Guides, tips and links to all things green.

www.celtnet.org

Center for Environmental Living and Training – The West of Ireland's charity for education and training in traditional and ecological skills.

www.green-england.co.uk

An online directory of green and ethical products, days out, services and information.

www.greenconsumerguide.com

This daily up-dated website provides environmental news and lists products and services.

Books for your Library

1001 Ways you can Save the Planet
by Joanna Yarrow, Published by Duncan Baird Publishers
ISBN: 978-1844833764

A Slice of Organic Life
Editor-in-Chief Sheherazade Goldsmith
Published by DK Publishing
ISBN: 978-0756662110

Dr. Pitcairn's Complete Guide to Natural Health for Dogs and Cats
by Richard H. Pitcairn and Susan Hubble Pitcairn
Published by Rodale Press
ISBN: 978-1579549732

Eco Dog: Healthy Living for Your Pet
by Corbett Marshall and Jim Deskevich
Published by Chronicle Books
ISBN: 978-0811860888

Go Mad! 365 Daily Ways to Save the Planet
Edited and compiled by The Ecologist
Published by Think Publishing
ISBN: 978-0954136307

Green Living for Dummies
by Liz Barclay and Michael Grosvenor
Published by John Wiley & Sons
ISBN: 978-0470060384

Holistic Guide for a Healthy Dog
by Wendy Volhard and Kerry Brown
Published by Howell Book House
ISBN: 978-1582451534

No Nettles Required
by Ken Thompson, Published by Eden Project Books
ISBN: 978-1905811144

Reduce, Reuse, Recycle
by Nicky Scott, Published by Chelsea Green Publishing
ISBN: 978-1933392752

The Lazy Girl's Guide to Green Living
by Anita Naik, Published by Piatkus Books
ISBN: 978-0749928261

The Little Book of Living Green
by Mark Hegarty, Published by Nightingale Press
ISBN: 978-1903222133

Trade Secrets: Cleaning
by Alexandra Fraser, Published by Orion
ISBN: 978-0752818177

Picture Credits

Index